796.357
HAR

How to Play Better Baseball

How to Play

EDITED BY JOEL H. COHEN

BUD HARRELSON

Better Baseball

NEW YORK   1972   ATHENEUM

Photographs by Nick Sorrentino

TO ALL THOSE WHO HELPED ME

THROUGHOUT MY CAREER

AND ESPECIALLY TO DON CURLEY,

MY COACH AT SUNSET HIGH SCHOOL

Contents

How to Play Better Baseball

A Word from Bud

BASEBALL IS ONE SPORT where size doesn't really matter. Ability is the only thing that counts.

It's to *you,* regardless of your size or ability or the extent of your baseball ambitions, that this book is addressed. The fact that you're reading this book means you're trying to upgrade your game. Of course, a book can't do any more than suggest ways of improving. You learn by doing, by playing, by constant practice. But it helps to play and practice the right way. So keep the tips you find here in mind.

Not all of the book is instruction. In many places I've merely given my experiences or the techniques I use in certain situations. You're smart enough to judge for yourself what lessons are to be learned, and what you can apply to your own play. Be careful, though: what works for a major-leaguer may be too advanced for amateur play. Besides, everyone has to find his own style, and what works for him. There are few pointers in baseball that are right for every player in every situation.

Take the advice of your coaches and managers, and use the suggestions that follow as a guide, not as a list of "musts."

In Little League, high school, Babe Ruth League, and college ball, I was hungry for advice, and stored up what I couldn't use immediately. You should do the same. Even if you don't use it now, some day you may want to go back to a way of playing that was suggested to you by someone who knew the game and cared about your development.

When you're trying to mold yourself as a ballplayer, you need all the help you can get. Your coach may be able to detect something that you're doing improperly and recommend a better way. It may not work out, but you'll never know until you try. If it fails, you'll still have learned something about yourself as a player, so in a sense there's no type of advice that's bad for anyone. The process of trial and error will tell you whether it's practical for you.

I figured the man giving me advice wanted to help me and the team. So I listened to my coaches and managers and got along with them. This helped me make it to the big leagues.

Taking advice wasn't always easy. But no manager

4

ever wanted me to be something I couldn't be, such as a productive RBI man. Some, though, wanted me to get on base more, and to try a different method of hitting. This was particularly true when I first started switch-hitting. At that time I was under Solly Hemus's guidance, and he wanted me to hit everything to left field. But when I got to the Mets, Gil Hodges wanted me to pull the ball occasionally. So I worked on it, and now I get a good percentage of my hits to right. Since I'm capable now of pulling the ball *or* hitting to the opposite field, pitchers are uncertain what to throw to me. It paid to take the advice.

Above all, keep in mind that baseball is a game, something to be enjoyed as an individual and as a member of a team. Have fun! And the best way to have fun at baseball—or anything else, for that matter —is to give it all you have, the best that's in you.

Now let's go to work on bringing out that best.

BUD HARRELSON

1. The Making of a Shortstop

T H E S H O R T S T O P generally has to be one of the fastest men on the ball club in order to be able to cover the far-flung territory assigned to him. He must have a good arm and good hands. If a shortstop is a good hitter, it's a bonus, but he *must* be a good fielder. That's his bread and butter.

It's different with other positions. For a third baseman, for instance, it's as important to hit well as it is to field. Tony Perez isn't one of the finest-fielding third basemen around, yet his job is secure because of his bat. Rico Petrocelli was a good shortstop, but he didn't cover as much territory as a man who ran better, so he was moved to third. Physical size also plays a part at third base. A big guy—say, 180 pounds—is a perfect third baseman, able to take that bad hop off the chest. Third-sackers should be able to use their bodies as a fielding tool, throw them in front of the ball to block it. The more size, weight, and muscle you have, the better you're able to withstand the shot. The majority of third basemen are big fellows with the necessary physical equipment to stop a liner with their bodies, and to hit the long ball. They should also be able to field slow-rolling bunts and make long, accurate throws across the diamond.

The first baseman doesn't need a good arm, but he's got to be able to handle all kinds of thrown balls—from hurried twisters that have to be "dug out" of the dirt to high sailers over his head. He has to know when to try to tag the runner, and he has to be fast on his feet, able to shift them for the best possible reach as he nabs a throw that's long or short or to one side of him.

He has to know when to try to make a putout on a ground ball unassisted or when he should throw to the pitcher covering first, when to go after a grounder hit to his right and when to leave it for the second baseman. Most of his catches on throws from the infield are two-handed, but, especially when he has to reach, he should be adept at catching with one hand.

He provides the target for other infielders to throw to, and it helps if he's tall. On throws that he has to make to other bases—say, on a first-to-second-to-first double play—it's an advantage if he's left-handed.

With a man on first or runners on first and third,

8

the first baseman "holds" a runner on by standing in front of the bag, ready to take a throw from the pitcher and sweep his glove to the ground to make a tag. When the pitcher starts to pitch, the first baseman generally takes a couple of steps toward second and assumes his normal defensive stance. On throws to the plate, the first baseman is the cutoff man on almost all plays except throws from the left fielder (see section on relays and cutoffs, page 63).

Mostly, however, the first baseman is depended on for long hits and RBIs. Many great hitters whose legs have lost the strength required for playing the outfield regularly have been moved to first base in the twilight of their careers. Mickey Mantle and Willie Mays are two examples.

A second baseman has to be able to cover territory, field batted balls cleanly, and make quick, short throws. He doesn't need as powerful an arm as a shortstop, but he does have to be quick because many of the balls he has to handle are slow bounding. He has to be capable of covering first on a bunt, and second as a pivot man on the double play.

The second baseman shares the responsibility with the shortstop for covering second on an attempted steal. He has to be able to pivot to his right when fielding a ball far from second when there is a chance of a force-out at second. And he has to be quick enough to take just about any grounder between second and first base.

The outfielders are usually the men who hit with power and drive in the runs. But there, too, you find exceptions. Matty Alou is left-handed, so he can't play second, third, or short (because he would have to make a pivot before throwing to first on almost every ground ball). And he's not tall enough to be a first baseman, so he has to play the outfield, even though he doesn't fulfill the RBI qualifications. One year, Matty was the league's leading hitter but had only 28 runs batted in. If someone like Lou Brock or Hank Aaron had that few RBIs, he'd be of considerably less value to his team.

On defense, outfielders obviously have to be able to cover a lot of territory, be able to run in and out to catch liners and high flies. Not only do they have to be sure-handed in catching flies, they have to know how to cut off or block hits, to prevent the batter and base runners from taking extra bases.

Different things are required for the three outfield positions. Since the center fielder has to cover the most territory, he's got to be the best in terms of speed and range, and he needs an accurate, powerful arm. Since most batters are right-handers who generally hit to the left side of second base, the left fielder gets more action than the right fielder and should be more capable, although it's hard to name many better outfielders than right fielder Henry Aaron. But because of the long throw from right field to third base, the right fielder needs a stronger arm than the left fielder.

There are those who consider it an advantage for the left fielder to throw right-handed, and the right fielder to throw left-handed.

I've always felt that managers of Little League and other amateur boys' teams should try to play a boy where he's happy playing. Of course, he can't put a left-handed thrower at shortstop (because of the time that would be wasted in pivoting to get in throwing position), but in general the manager should try to play the fellow where he wants to play. On the other hand, you, the ballplayer, should be willing to play anywhere your coach or manager wants you to play, whether it's your favorite position or not.

\ Before I became a shortstop, I played third, second, the outfield and pitcher—wherever they put me. I was so small a lot of people didn't want me to play, period, but I had so much desire that I took any position I could get.

I'd been playing for two years at third base for my high school coach, and in my junior year had a good chance of making all-league or all-county for our school district as a third baseman. But that season my coach asked me, "Would you play shortstop instead of third base?" and I said, "Sure," because now I was faster and had a better arm than our first-string shortstop. As it turned out, I did make all-league that junior year—as a shortstop.

My high school success at short didn't establish me there for good, though. In college I went out for baseball and, when I said I played shortstop, juniors and seniors on the team said, "Oh-oh." They explained the team's shortstop was a senior who'd been playing the position since his freshman year. "You're in trouble," they said. "The coach likes him, and I doubt you can come in and move him out." So I asked, "Where *can* I play?" and was told, "Third base." So I did try out for third and won the job, playing my freshman year there. Funny thing is, I signed my professional contract as a shortstop after the scouts had seen me play third. But they knew I was a shortstop.

Should *you* be a shortstop? First consider the responsibilities that go with the position and then the skills that are involved, and decide for yourself.

In the field, my job is to make the key plays, avoid errors, more or less run the infield, be smart, and take advantage of my speed. You need speed to range as wide as a shortstop must. But fast or not, I think the top-rated shortstops are those with very strong arms; the fellows who are just average are that way because of their so-so arms. They don't make the double play; they can't make up for lost time. For instance, if a ball isn't hit that well and the throw comes to the shortstop from the pitcher or second baseman a little late, he can't make up for the slowness of the play if he doesn't have a good arm.

When a ballplayer talks about someone having good hands, he means that everything he gets to he catches. But without a good arm, a shortstop won't rise above average, no matter what kind of hands he has. There are certainly men in the league who have better hands than I do, but who aren't as fast or equipped with as good an arm. Chances are they make their errors because their arm isn't really adequate to rifle the ball in time to get the runner on a close play. And because of that weakness, accuracy may be lacking as well.

Can a young player develop these skills? Definitely yes. Every day you'll hear the statement that a particular player is blessed with certain inborn ability. Willie Mays is a good example—he has so much natural ability he can make the toughest catches hardly without having to think about it. But there are other fellows who don't have anywhere near the natural speed or arm that Willie has, they're nowhere nearly the coordinated runner he is, and yet they are fine fielders because they work at it constantly.

Brooks Robinson, for instance, is a very slow man. He doesn't have an outstandingly good arm, but he has splendid reflexes and hands. You know that it didn't come overnight; he had to have taught himself. In fact, Brooks has said that when he first came up he was a second baseman and was moved to third because the decision makers didn't think he was a good-enough second baseman for the major leagues. What better thing could have happened for him and his ball club? Possibly it was because of the people he had around him that he was so successful at the hot corner, but to be considered a so-so second baseman, and then such a good third baseman, means he had worked and worked.

Even for people with natural ability, there's a lot of work involved in becoming outstanding. Throughout my minor-league career I knew fellows who had much better natural ability than I did, but they just weren't hungry to excel, so they never made it. They thought they'd win out by just going out there and doing their thing, whereas I knew I had to concentrate and practice, practice, practice. I used to take hundreds of ground balls every day, hour after hour, until I couldn't stand up. It's paid off.

I didn't always have a good arm, but I worked with it, and it got a little stronger each year. By the time I was in high school, I was able to throw the ball quite hard. Constant practice did it.

The point is, regardless of what ability you're born with, you still have to work on it. The less natural skill you have, the harder you have to work. But no matter how much or little you start with, you *can* develop the abilities that go into becoming a better baseball player.

KNOW YOURSELF

Basically, it's a matter of taking advantage of what you have. Don't try to be what you're not; don't try to be what you have no chance of becoming.

In the minor leagues, I discovered the truth of this advice. I knew I had good legs and could see the ball well and make contact, and I knew the pitcher wouldn't be able to strike me out as easily as he could a lot of other players. But I also knew some things I couldn't do, like long-distance power hitting. I knew I wasn't going to hit fifty home runs a year—in the majors, I've hit just two, and one of them inside the park—so I didn't try to kid myself. I couldn't be what I wasn't, and I knew that, in order to play and to stay, I had to learn certain things to get on base, such as developing my swing to try and hit the ball on the ground. It meant not trying to be the hero. It's nice to be one— to be strong and hit a home run and win the game— but that's not me. My job is to get on base, whether it's by a walk or bunt or maybe a slap hit, and let somebody else hit it out to win. Then I've done my job and he's done his.

Analyze your skills—and be honest with yourself. Decide what you're capable of doing or becoming, and get to work at it.

If you're lucky enough to live where the climate is warm all year, try to play baseball all year. But if, like most people, your baseball season is limited, try to play at other sports during the rest of the year, because they, too, will help your baseball. The playing's the thing.

I had the advantage of growing up in California, and during my high school days, first at Hayward and then at Sunset, I played baseball twelve months a year. While school was in session, I played for the school team. During the summer, it was American Legion ball, and then, in the fall, semipro ball on Saturdays and Sundays. This still left time for football and basketball, which I played, even though I wanted to make baseball a career, because I'd been on those teams in past years and still felt an obligation. They helped me in baseball. In fact, I think the jumping ability and quickness they developed really meant the difference between being a mediocre shortstop and a good one.

As an example, at five feet, eight inches in high school, I got to the point where I could jump and get my full hand above the rim of the basket. Football taught me how to be quick on my feet and how to back-pedal, both valuable skills for a shortstop. As a halfback—they were skinny in those days—I led the league in pass receiving. Trying to catch passes had to help my hands in some respects, since it involves coordination of hands and eyes, and, thanks to my football pass-catching experience, I can go back into the outfield and catch a pop-up over my shoulder with relative ease, something a lot of infielders find awfully difficult to do.

So play *something*. And try to win.

To win, you have to want very much to win. You have to develop a sense of competition. On the other hand, having tried your best, you shouldn't think that

16

because you lost, *all* is lost. Too often the managers of boys' baseball teams put the wrong emphasis on winning. They play to win, which is as it should be, but instead of just teaching the boys *how* to win, they seem to teach that winning is everything. That's wrong, because life isn't all winning, either. You've got to accept the downs with the ups.

Sports teach you to compete, which is a quality that's all-important in almost any phase of life. If you don't know how to contend for something you want, more often than not you'll end up being a loser, no matter how intelligent you are.

EQUIPMENT IS PART OF THE CONFIDENCE GAME (A GLOVE SHOULD FIT—LIKE A GLOVE)

Regardless of what sport you're playing, the confidence factor is crucial. Part of it is having confidence in your equipment. If you feel, for example, that your glove is flimsy or that the ball isn't going to stay in it because it's hard or not big enough, that's surely going to affect your fielding. You'll be worrying about your glove when your only concern should be catching the ball. I know the feeling from recent experience. The strings on my glove had been tightened too much during the 1970 season, and a line drive off Pete Rose's bat on a hit-and-run broke them. I ran in and got someone else's, but the rest of the game I had the feeling it didn't fit right.

So get a glove you'll be happy with, even if you have to buy it yourself. A lot of parents don't realize the importance of it and are content to get their children just any glove. Why not earn your own money and get yourself the equipment you know will do the job? I bought myself my first thirty-five-dollar glove before high school with money I had worked for and saved because I always wanted to use the best equipment. But no matter what you pay for a glove, and whatever the brand name, make sure you get one you can handle.

If you've worked to buy your glove, you're more likely to be proud of it, the way I was. Even as a youngster, I never had a glove lost or stolen, because I carried it with me. I was proud of what I had.

The glove isn't going to make the player, but it helps to have a good glove with a nice pocket that you can work with. Keep it oiled (there's a special glove oil you can use) and take care of it. Don't throw your glove into the dirt, because dirt will eventually make it hard.

Some players, when they first get a glove, tie a couple of baseballs in it, throw it into the whirlpool, and soak it. I don't. Chances are I'll let Yogi Berra use it a week throwing in batting practice, just to loosen it up. I like to break in a glove gradually. I'll use one glove to take ground balls with before a game, and save one glove for the game. (The same thing with a bat. I don't use a game bat during practice.)

Once a glove is broken in, I try to keep it tight. I'm constantly tightening it up because the rawhide does stretch, causing the glove to get a little flimsy and flap all over. Stretched rawhide made Dave Marshall flinch once when he caught a drive. The ball almost came through his glove between two fingers and would have hit him.

Just as a glove should fit your hand, socks and shoes should fit your feet. If you're a size 8, don't buy size 9½ baseball spikes because you want them to last three years and expect to grow into them. Speaking of big feet, I remember that, when I was scouted in high school, a scout looked at the big clodhoppers on my small body and said, "Those spikes don't fit you." He was concerned because he didn't want me to ruin my feet. I put my foot up and he felt my toe and agreed the shoes fit. "Boy," he said, "you're gonna be a big ballplayer when you grow into your feet." Between you and me, I had the feeling that when they signed me to a professional contract, they thought I was going to grow into my shoes—but I never did.

GETTING READY

Okay, you've got your equipment—your good-fitting glove and spikes—and you've made the team. Now, how are you going to make sure you stick?

The obvious answer is practice. But practice what? In my opinion, a player is wise to concentrate on his weaknesses. Sure, it's more fun to do what you're best at, in spring training or pregame drills. But that's not going to help you where you need it most. I've noticed major-leaguers who are good in hitting but very weak at certain other things and yet, since they never really work on their weaknesses, they never improve.

The toughest position to work on is catching, if for no other reason than that it's so tiring, but it can still be done. A bad defensive catcher who doesn't play regularly should catch batting practice—and not wait to be asked. We had a catcher who could have improved his defensive work, but he just stood around the batting cage. He's no longer with us.

I'd rather spend time on something I need a lot of work on—such as backhanding a ball—than just go out with no objective but to get loose. When I have no particular fielding problem, I'll try to take more swings in batting practice.

You should lay down the groundwork in the spring for how you're going to work out during the season. (I'm not talking about calisthenics, which we do all spring training. Once the season begins, the day-to-day bending over and fielding are enough to keep our muscles toned.) In their own way, pregame warm-ups are as important as spring training. It's vital that you warm up properly.

A lot of boys will go out and play without warming up correctly. For example, let's say they're having a catch. A boy will catch the ball in front of his face and throw it from there. Then he'll bend over to catch one at his knees, and he'll straighten up and throw the same way as when he caught the first one up high. But in a game you don't always have time to straighten up and throw from the top; you might have to get the ball away like a submarine pitcher, the quickest way you can. What may happen to the boy who keeps throwing from a straight-up position during warm-up is that the first time in the game he has to backhand a ball and make a sidearm throw, he rips an arm muscle. It wouldn't have happened if he had warmed up with all kinds of throws, so that he gradually stretched the muscle.

My philosophy is that you should warm up as if you're actually playing the game. Throwing a baseball isn't a natural motion—that's why players develop sore arms and arthritis and bursitis—so to get your arm in shape, whether you're a pitcher, outfielder, or infielder, you have to practice throwing from all positions.

Some youngsters ruin themselves for life in boys' leagues, but not if they're properly coached. My coach preached this to me: "If you catch the ball waist-high, throw it from the waist. If you catch it on the right side, don't straighten up and throw overhand, throw from the side."

21

Put a lot into your warm-up because I'm convinced you're going to play the way you warm up. If you warm up with a nonchalant attitude, you're going to play that way.

Usually I throw with Jerry Grote, our catcher, just before I go out to take infield practice. To start with, I just toss the ball softly from a short distance, and keep taking a step back about every two or three throws. I gradually throw harder and harder, and, when I think I am properly warm, I throw as hard as I possibly can because I know that when I get in a game there will be times when I have to throw it that hard.

Sometimes in warm-up I'll throw the ball to the point that my arm actually aches, but all that means is that I've really stretched the muscles, and that, since I'm properly loose, I won't tear one. Having thrown as hard as I can, I know I'm ready. I may not throw that hard during infield practice, because I'm already loose and I don't want to overdo it. I want to save something for the game.

Obviously, there's no substitute for playing every day to keep yourself in top playing condition. The less you play, the more attention you have to pay to conditioning. You have to make sure your arms and legs get loose, especially in cool weather. And you have to guard against overdoing your warm-up. That's why there are some days I get loose and skip infield practice.

22

2. On the Field

IT'S TIME to take the field.

You trot out to shortstop, whip the ball around the infield, and set yourself for the first batter. But where? The saying that position is everything in life is true for baseball defense, too. It's a complex matter. The inning, the score, who's hitting, how he's hitting, how fast he runs, who's pitching, the game situation, and how good your arm is, all have a bearing on where you locate yourself.

In the major leagues, a shortstop knows the hitters, what pitches they hit where, and what the capabilities of his pitchers are. Of course, the pitchers change; they

23

get more tired as a game progresses and as the season progresses. So you have to adjust accordingly.

If you know Hank Aaron is a pull hitter, you play him that way. But if you feel your pitcher isn't throwing as hard as he should, you might have to play a step *more* toward third base than you would normally. How deep or shallow you have to play depends on how the batter runs. For a Lou Brock, you have to be a little closer in toward the pitching mound than for a fellow like Joe Torre, who doesn't run that well.

All these things are involved in professional ball, but you can't be too smart in Little League because the hitters aren't that predictable. They're not polished enough to hit consistently one way, so that, as a fielder, you can't safely assume that, because a player hit to left field last time at bat, he'll do it again this time.

You can try to analyze different opposing batters, though, to pick up little inside tips about them. I like to watch opposing hitters in batting practice because they change so much from time to time. Sometimes they're not swinging the bat well, they're getting jammed, and they're smart enough to know that maybe they're lunging at the ball, or they're swinging too much out in front, so they'll try to hit the ball up the middle. A pull hitter who's struggling will probably be trying to hit the ball up the middle, so you have to position yourself accordingly.

I like to move around a lot on a batter. If a man hits a ball hard to my right and I make the play, he's not go-

24

ing to be too anxious to hit the same way next time, so I anticipate that. Many times I've been able to rob a guy to my right; then he hits one sharply up the middle and I get that one, too. Now I've really got him. He's likely to be so confused he may not be able to hit any pitch thrown up there.

At the 1970 All-Star game, Clarence Gaston of San Diego and Roberto Clemente, the great Pirate star, were talking about me and laughing. Clarence had been telling Roberto how I just about drove him up the wall by changing position on him. I remembered one game where he hit a ball up the middle and I was able to get to it and throw him out. Then, the next time he was at bat, I saw that a curve was being called for. I know he pulls the breaking ball, so I stepped more toward third. Sure enough, he hit the next pitch on the ground right to me.

"You've robbed me eight times already," he said.

"That's my job," I said, appreciative of the compliment he was paying me.

A word of caution: I attempt anticipating where the ball is going to be hit *only* if there's no great loss if the batter should cross me up. Guess right and you're a hero; guess wrong and—well, it's no sin, unless you were ridiculously out of position. Baseball is a game of odds, and that's what positioning is. You figure what's *likely* to happen, and move on that basis.

I often change position during the same at-bat, because a man with a 2–0 count on him is more likely

25

to get his pitch to pull than if he has a 1–1 count. Being ahead of the pitcher, why should he look for a ball away when he can wait for a pitch, inside or over the plate, that he can pull?

On the other hand, if, say, Tom Seaver is ahead of a man who's a pull hitter, he's not going to give him anything to pull. If the batter does try to pull, he'll hit the ball straight at you or up the middle, and with no authority, because he'd been looking for an inside pitch and got one that was away.

Which side of the plate a man hits from, of course, influences where you position yourself defensively. More right-handed hitters hit the ball to right field than left-handed batters hit to left, a main reason for this being that a ball hit to right field advances a man more easily than one hit to left. So I usually play closer to second base on left-handed batters, more so than I play closer to *third* base on right-handed hitters.

Unless the man is a definite, deadly pull hitter, I don't like to play a lot to my right, because that's the toughest play to make. Nine times out of ten you won't be able to throw the man out on a ball hit deep to the hole anyway, so you might as well make certain you'll be in position to get the ball hit to your left. A right-hander generally hits with authority when he pulls the ball, while, if he hits it up the middle, he may just stroke it. This is more likely to happen when he has two strikes on him, because then he's just trying to make contact and probably won't be himself and pull. This emphasizes how worthwhile it is to change position on a man even during the same at-bat, since the pitching strategy changes with the count, and so does the batter's intent.

In a mid-season 1971 game against the Reds, I must have changed position four times on Johnny Bench in one at-bat. I knew he'd look to pull the first pitch—he certainly wasn't going to hit a soft grounder up the middle—so I moved to my right, being more willing to take chances with nobody on. It was a strike. I figured the pitcher would be throwing away from Bench on the next pitch, so I moved to my left. Ball one. Then another ball, making the count 2–1, so I went back to my right, figuring Bench would be trying to pull again, and the pitcher wouldn't be trying to waste one with that count. It was a strike, so, with the count now 2–2, I moved somewhere in between.

Here's my reasoning: On a first pitch, a good hitter is going to be aggressive and willing to be fooled because, even if he misses, he's only down one strike. But if he's got two strikes on him, he'll tend to wait a little longer on a pitch, so he can handle anything that comes at him, be it a breaking ball, a fast ball away, or whatever is thrown. In danger of striking out, he'll just try to hit the ball where it's pitched. Often, he'll swing at an outside pitch that he should be trying to hit to right field and try to pull it, with the result that he hits it up the middle. So that's why I adjusted as I did.

Generally, when no one is on base the infield plays

back in "normal" position. With men on base, in scoring position, I tend to play a little deeper, so that if the batter does hit it well, I can knock it down. I might not throw anyone out, but at least I might keep them from scoring.

There are times when you try to accomplish the same thing by having the infield "in." This means you play maybe twenty feet closer to the plate than you would normally. It works about half the time. Sometimes it psychs the batter to see everyone standing on top of him. He knows he has to hit the ball hard, so he overswings and pops it up. But, on the other hand, this alignment might allow a .200 hitter to bloop a single over you, a single that would have been an easy out if you were at your normal playing depth. And, with the infield in, any ball hit with some power and not right at you is a base hit.

But when there's an enemy runner at third and your team is behind, it's important to try to cut that run off, so you take the chance. The same thing applies late in the game, if the score is tied or the teams are within a run of each other.

In a situation where a double play is a good possibility, the shortstop and second baseman are back, but not quite as deep as they play normally. Generally, with a right-handed batter the shortstop comes up about five steps closer to the plate and a couple of steps to his left; for a left-handed batter, the infield shifts somewhat more to right field.

In a double-play situation, the reason you have to come in and over is that, if the ball is hit back to the pitcher, you can get back in time to cover. Often, when the second baseman is covering, I take a chance that the batter is not going to try just to hit the ball, but to hit it with authority. A Hank Aaron will almost always hit it to the shortstop's right, so, because he usually hits the ball sharply and he runs well, I may move a step or two to the right of my normal double-play depth, or stay straight away. I vary as much as twenty feet in where I stand on different right-hand hitters.

Where the other infielders play depends on circumstances, and there are all sorts of combinations. If, say, there are men on first and third and one out, and you can afford to give up a run if need be, the first and third basemen play in, ready either to cut down the run or to try for a double play on a hard-hit ball.

If there is nobody out with runners on first and third, I'd be halfway between in and back. The reason is that, with no outs, the runner on third is going to make absolutely certain the ball is through before he runs. There's no reason for him to take an unnecessary chance when there's still the possibility of a sacrifice fly. Similarly, a slow runner like John Bateman is not going to try to score with less than two outs unless he's sure the ball is hit through. And if you're the Giants and you've got Willie McCovey, with two bad legs, on third base, you'd want him to *walk* home. The shortstop can help make sure the runner is a base sticker by moving in temporarily. Seeing this, the coach will advise the runner, "Make it be through." Then, with the runner staying close to third, you move back to double-play position.

In addition, with men on first and third there's no reason for the lead runner, especially if he's not agile, to risk getting into a rundown so the man on first can go to second.

I depend on the hitter to tell me where the ball is going to be hit. He doesn't mean to, but in most instances he lets you know what he's up to by certain giveaway signals. In order to hit an outside pitch, you have to keep your hips closed and go into the ball; when you're going to pull the ball, you open up your hips and start getting the bat out over the plate. So he telegraphs his intention, and you can "cheat" by anticipating where you think he'll hit it and start shifting your weight in that direction. Of course, you can be fooled, too, especially if the pitcher fools him and he can't hit it where he planned to. But that happens only once in maybe twenty-five times, so again you have to go with the odds.

To sum up, you should position yourself according to the capabilities of the man at bat, what he's done before and what he's likely to do now. You also have to consider how your pitcher is doing, what the count is, the situation in the inning, and the score of the game. Don't be afraid to take chances, but make sure the risks don't outweigh the possible advantages.

HANDLING GROUNDERS

Like most new players, when I first came into the major leagues I just about prayed that I wouldn't be the "goat," the fellow who made the error that cost my team the game. In crucial situations I'd hope the ball would be hit somewhere else besides shortstop. This is no way to approach the game, of course—you should be confident—but it's the way it was. And even after I'd been in the majors a couple of seasons, there were occasional flickers of that old feeling.

During the 1969 season, though, in one game we were ahead of the Giants by one run. In the ninth inning, they had men at first and third and Willie Mays coming to the plate.

"Oh, well," I told myself, "here comes a sacrifice fly—or worse." But then I had a second thought: "Wait a minute. Willie's human. Maybe he'll hit a double-play ball to me and we'll get out of the inning with a victory." That's exactly what happened.

Now, I'm certainly not suggesting that it was ESP that got Willie to hit it to me. Wishing *won't* make it so. But the point is, I'd reached the level where I was not only willing to have the ball hit to me in a critical situation, but eager for it. And, when that happens to you, you'll know you've arrived as far as self-confidence in your fielding is concerned. In turn, that feeling will help your fielding. Just put it to work. . . .

You take your position and set yourself comfort-

31

Picture ABOVE *shows the basic stance as the pitch starts toward the plate. In picture* BELOW *the ball is getting closer to the plate. Come up on your toes so you can be ready to move in either direction. You want to be moving on the ball when it's hit to you.*

ably. Probably you're in a slight crouch, with knees slightly bent, feet spread comfortably, ready to move in any direction with the crack of the bat. Your hands rest on your knees or in front of them, waiting. As the pitch comes in, your weight shifts slightly forward and you lean in, on the balls of your feet.

The pitch is thrown, the batter connects, and the ball is bounding in your direction. What you should do—unless it's a line drive or pop fly—is move toward the ball. A lot of youngsters are reluctant to do that, and end up fielding the ball somewhere in between hops instead of nabbing it at the top of the bounce, where it should be taken. When that happens, they take a step in and start leaning backwards, and all the fundamentals of fielding fall apart. They're back on their heels, off balance, and in no position to bend over and extend their arms fully.

So go after the ball. Be aggressive. Keep in mind that you're the master out there. The ball isn't chasing you; you're chasing it, and you're going to field it without hesitation.

If it's hit hard and directly at you, come in on it and set yourself with feet spread, right foot slightly behind the left. Your body should be low, back fairly straight and knees bent, eyes constantly on the ball.

On a slow-hit ground ball, put on the speed and keep your body low. Get the glove on the ground well in front of you and let the ball roll into it. There may be times when the only chance you'll have to get the

33

This is the correct way to field a ground ball. Keep the glove in front of your body and your head down. You should be able to see the ball rolling into the glove. Your bare hand should then reach in to get the ball out.

runner is to pick the ball up barehanded. With practice, you'll learn to do it with your body a little to the left of the ball.

On a ground ball hit with any speed, however, it's important to get in front of it, if at all possible. The reason is simple: if a grounder takes a bad hop or you misjudge it, your body is a tool for stopping the ball, whatever position you're playing. Many young players have the habit of reaching down with their glove hand and fielding the ball to the side. But that way, if the ball should come up three inches or veer to the side, they won't have any way of stopping it. If you're where you should be in relation to the ball, though, often it will hit you in the chest or leg and fall in front of you, and you will still have a shot at getting the man at first. So, instead of an error or bad-hop single to the outfield, it's an out—and that's why I like to get in front of most every ball. The exception is the one that hits two feet in front with enough force to go through the outfield wall. Like anyone else, I'm afraid of being killed or breaking a bone, so I might flinch.

But, generally, you try to get in front of every ball. And you position yourself so that you're catching it out in front of you, where you can see the ball heading for the glove, not back between your legs. If you catch it with your hands out in front of you, you can see how much the ball is above or below your glove, and adjust. If you bend over enough and get close enough to the ground, you can almost see the ball roll

This is the wrong way to field a ground ball.
The glove is back too far and the eyes are
not on the ball.

into the glove. You're bending over, letting the ball come into the glove instead of jabbing at the ball, and now everything is easy. And as a rule it's better to stay low, because it's easier to come up on a surprise bounce than suddenly swoop down.

Most ground balls are fielded below the belt, so your fingers should be pointing down, the pinkies of bare hand and glove should be close together, and your palms should be facing the ball. Elbows and hands should be away from your body. (It helps to practice with someone rolling the ball toward you.) When the ball hops high above the belt, the way to field it is with the fingers pointing upward and thumbs close together. The bare hand serves to help trap the ball in the glove.

When fielding a low bouncing ball below the waist, keep your fingers down, little fingers touching to form a cup. Use your bare hand to guide the ball into the glove.

When fielding a high bouncing ball above the waist, keep your bare hand below the glove, so if the ball falls out your hand will be in position to retrieve it.

Again, of course, the palms are facing the ball.

One of the things that make playing shortstop interesting and difficult is the obvious fact that many grounders are hit to the side of you. Wherever possible on such plays you still want to try to get in front of the ball, and as fast as you can. Again, keep your body low and watch the ball as you run. Don't try to time it—get there so you can play it as if it were hit straight at you. If the ball is hard hit to your side, either cut straight across or go diagonally back to get it. If it's hit to your side but only medium hard, run in for it diagonally. If it's slow hit to the side, run to it fast. It's all pretty much common sense.

When you're running to your left and you have no time to get in front of the ball, you have to field it on the run, which means sometimes you can't get set for the throw to first. What you should try to do is brake yourself, make the throw off your right foot, and step in the direction of first with your left.

When you have to go to your right for a ball, you're running in the opposite direction of where your throw will be. This means you have to stop in front of the ball by jamming your right foot against the ground, pivoting on it, and stepping toward first with your left foot as you make the throw.

There are times when the chance of making a putout is small, but it's important that the ground ball not get through you. (This applies even more to outfielders than infielders, since a ball that gets through an out-

Improper start in going after a ground ball.

This is a good start. The crossover step should be used. Right foot over left in going to the left, and left foot over right in going to the right. The bat shows where the first step brings you when you start off on the wrong foot. You cover twice the distance by using the crossover step. In fielding, the first step is the most important, and will determine if you can reach the ball.

fielder will often result in a run.) If the conventional way of fielding the particular grounder involves too much risk of this happening, there are two ways to block the ball. In one, the heels are kept together so that the feet form a V. In the other, the fielder places one knee on the ground and the ball is caught where the knee and foot meet. Infielders generally prefer the heels-together method, with the feet at almost a right angle and the ball taken nearer the heels, providing it's a grounder.

The points to remember about fielding grounders are: Set yourself comfortably and up on the balls of your feet, ready to move in any direction. Be aggressive; move toward the ball and grab it at the top of the bounce. Whenever possible, get in front of the ball so, in case of a bad hop or misjudgment, your body will stop it. Stay low, keep your eyes on the ball, and try to have it come to you instead of jabbing at it. Field the ball with your hands out in front of you so you can see the ball heading for the glove. And remember, even on the tough ones hit to your side, you, not the ball, are the master.

It's probably different for some shortstops, but for most of us the most difficult play to handle is the ball hit toward the shortstop's right, in the hole between short and third. That has to be a backhand play, which is tough in itself. Then, if you make the grab, you still need to get the ball away in a hurry and make a good, strong, accurate throw.

On a ball hit to your backhand, use a crossover step and put your glove into position immediately. Let the ball come to the glove rather than stabbing at the ball with the glove.

The play is especially tough if the ball hit to your right is down. In that case you're bending over, and, aside from everything else, you have to field it bending over, then straighten up, stop, and throw. (On a ball hit to your right at shortstop, you have to straighten up because there's no way you can go toward third base and make an underhand throw to first with any accuracy or momentum.) Just about your only chance to get a man on that kind of play is if you're lucky enough to have had a man on first. Then you can flip the ball back to second for the force. In the 1971 World Series, Mark Belanger of the Baltimore Orioles went to his right for a ball and just managed to force the Pittsburgh Pirates' Manny Sanguillen at second.

Any more than an outfielder can perfect diving catches, there's little you can do to work on that kind of play, except take a lot of ground balls and hope that a good many are the type that go that way.

Some players are better at handling a ball hit down to their right than others. Roy McMillen, for instance, always stayed real low. And he didn't run the way I do. Often, I'll get a ball backhand, but I'm running at full speed past the third baseman and then I have to make a throw all the way across the infield. Half the time I can't even stop, so I just hold on to the ball. With a slow runner at the plate, I can sometimes circle around behind the ball and come back in to grab it for an easy play, rather than backhand it the way some shortstops do when they don't have to. I never backhand a ball on the dead run unless it's an absolute must. It's much easier to get something on your throw to first if you're somewhat in front of the ball when you take it.

Sometimes a very easy play can prove tough, but the toughest is invariably the one you have to backhand.

GRIPPING THE BALL

Through practice, you get the feel of where you like to have the ball in your hand as you throw. I like to hold the ball across the seams with my index and mid-

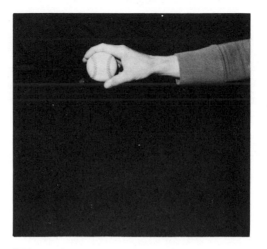

When throwing, grip the ball this way, across the seams. Keep the ball away from your palms.

dle fingers on top and close together. This way, I get equal pressure on both fingers and at the same spot. You don't always get the ball out of your glove that way, but when you have time you can always turn the ball a little bit, by feel, to where it's most comfortable for you. (Some players have thrown the ball into the dugout because the glove they were reaching into was too large and they couldn't find "the handle.") With equal seams on both sides of your fingers, you don't have to grip bare rawhide and the ball has more of a tendency to go true to first base.

Many young ballplayers grip the ball real tight, and as a result can't use their wrist to throw. You can't squeeze the ball and throw well, so you should just relax. Grip it up toward the front—between the thumb and the first two fingers—and hold it very loosely, just letting the ball roll off your fingertips. If you hold it in the back of your hand, you get what we call a "palm ball," and you're actually pushing it, rather than throwing it.

MAKING THE THROW

The key to throwing well is your wrist. The snap of the wrist is the end of the whiplike motion that your arm and body go through as you throw. People say to me, "You're not built very big and you're not very strong looking, and yet you throw hard." I think it's just a matter of good wrist action. I also have the advantage of not being overly muscular to the point that I'm restricted in throwing. I'm very wiry as far as being able to move my arm is concerned, so I'm getting more arm speed as well as having good wrist action.

How far I move my arm back in making a throw depends on the particular throw I'm making. A lot of times I throw right from my ear. It's just a quick flip. When there's more time, I bring my arm back like the pitcher would and throw over the top. This puts less strain on your arm than when you drop down to throw. You can get more body into it.

Young players ask if they should straighten up to make the throw. Well, each shortstop is different. I

44

The overhand throw—the most accurate and powerful throw.

would hate to tell a Gene Michaels type of shortstop, one who is six-four, that he has to stand straight up. This takes him longer than it takes me, and that extra instant might be the difference between a base hit and a putout.

How much time you have to make the play will determine whether or not you straighten up, and, to a certain extent, it will establish what kind of throw you should make. In any case, don't throw the ball until you have it.

If you have to get the throw away very quickly, and have no time to straighten up, you may have to throw underhand. For short, quick throws, a sidearm delivery can be used, but the most accurate and powerful is the overhand.

The three-quarter throw. Use this one more for short throws. Make sure you get the left side of your body out of the way so the person receiving the throw can have full sight of the ball.

The submarine throw. Use this when you have to throw the ball in a hurry. Keep your glove out of the way so it does not block the throw or the view of the person you are throwing to.

Generally, though, it depends on the individual. Some shortstops throw three-quarters better than they do overhand or sidearm. With others, overhand is their best throw, and so on. I would tell you what I told one of our new players when he first came up. He had time to make the play, and he made a little flip throw that sank and was into the dirt. As it turned out he got the man anyway, but he had made what amounted to an unnecessarily daring throw. I told him, "When you have time, make your best throw, whichever it is."

The reverse problem is taking too much time on a throw and then throwing it harder than necessary. Chris Speier, the Giants' shortstop, has to learn to overcome this tendency. In the National League 1971 playoffs, Dave Cash hit a two-hop ground ball to Speier. Chris, who's noted for his arm, took three steps before he threw and just barely retired Dave.

When most young infielders first come up, they want to throw every ball hard to first. If they would only realize their arms can withstand only so many hard throws a year, just as a pitcher can throw only so many fast balls a game. Hard throws are more tiring, they take more effort, and you have more chance of hurting your arm. So, when you don't have to, don't throw harder than necessary. Save it for when you need it.

Often you need it when you're trying for a double play. If I've got time on a d.p. attempt, I throw directly over the top, because that's where I throw the hardest from, and my ball doesn't sink or slide. If I throw the ball submarine style, like a relief pitcher with a good sinker ball, it's tougher for the first baseman to catch it. So use your best throw whenever possible.

Hector Torres, who backs up Don Kessinger, was with Fresno in the California League when I was out there. He used to make a three-quarter throw from the hole—the only way he could throw well—and to me it looked unorthodox. But there's no such thing as unorthodox, if it works for you. If it's the best throw you can make with something on it, and you have more accuracy doing it that way, then by all means use it.

You shouldn't have to take a lot of steps to throw hard. One should do it. And you shouldn't waste your hard throws.

CALLING FOR THE BALL

Pop flies seem to give infielders more trouble than anything else. I used to have trouble with pop flies, but I just went out and worked on the problem until I had it under control. After a while you get the feeling, though wind conditions can make the ball drift and occasionally you get fooled.

In the 1971 All-Star game in Detroit, on a very windy day, a ball was hit up in the air to short left field.

48

I broke back for it and the left fielder hustled in, but the wind caught it and I had to go all the way back to shortstop—where I'd come from—to make the catch.

Judging high pops comes with practice. When a ball goes up, many youngsters like to keep the ball way in front of them, but what usually happens then is that it *falls* in front of them. I like to have the feeling that the ball is going to hit me right on the head, and I position my body accordingly, getting under it when it's at the top of its arc.

It's a must that you call, "I've got it," or signal for a fly ball in order to avoid collisions and make sure that the ball is caught. On an infield pop that doesn't go much past the plate, it should be the first or third baseman who makes the catch. The catcher will often wheel around to get a good angle on the ball and either snare it himself or help direct traffic. Sometimes the pitcher has to help call whose ball it is. In the 1971 All-Star game, Joe Torre, the third baseman, called for a ball that went up toward him, and Willie McCovey, who had started in, went back to first. Torre yelled, "I've got it," and I was yelling, "Torre, Torre, Torre." So was the pitcher. But meanwhile the wind was blowing the ball almost back to first, and it really wasn't the third baseman's ball any more. But the reason Torre stayed with it—and caught it about ten feet from first—was that everyone was yelling for him to take it and nobody called him off. So he kept going, right over the top of the mound, and made the catch.

On a ball popped shallow to the outfield, on which an outfielder has as good a shot at catching it as the infielder, the outfielder should take it, because he's coming toward the ball. Often you don't know which of you will take it until the last instant, especially when you, the infielder, are running with your back to the ball.

In situations like that, I turn around and look, and if I think I've got it, I put one hand up in the air and wave it, to let the outfielder know I'm going to make the catch. I don't yell anything in a case like that because, with all the crowd noise and since I'm not facing him, he probably wouldn't be able to hear me. But the outfielder running in and watching the ball can see the infielder's hand go up. If the outfielder is convinced he himself can catch it, he can yell, "I've got it," and the infielder will probably hear him, since he's heading in the outfielder's direction.

In one game, midway through the 1971 season, I got run over by our left fielder on a pop fly. He yelled, "I've got it," all right—and I heard him—but it was too late for me to get out of the way. Also, if I had quit on the ball, he might have stopped short to avoid running into me and the ball would have dropped. So we collided—but I caught the ball. I'd rather be hit than quit on a ball. On those close ones when collisions are a possibility, I brace myself so that, if we do happen to hit, I can still hold onto the ball.

Of course, you try to prevent collisions, and it's

The proper way to catch a pop-up. Call for the ball so the outfielder can see you. Keep your hands high as the ball is coming down.

usually just a matter of one man calling the other off. Say I've signaled for a pop and Dave Marshall, racing in from the outfield, yells, "I've got it, I've got it." I'll get out of the way and turn around and yell "Take it, take it." (If I had yelled, "You've got it," he might not have heard the "you've" and guessed that I was yelling *I* would take it.) Or I might yell, "Dave, Dave," and hope it's not Cleon or another fielder coming in.

Sometimes you can get fooled. We were playing in one of the ball parks where the bullpen is halfway down the line, right on the playing field (in foul territory). A ball was popped up along the line, toward the left-field corner, and I back-pedaled for it.

I was just starting to reach up for the ball when I heard a voice that sounded like Cleon's yell, "I've got it, I've got it." So I quit on the ball. But it wasn't Cleon who had called for it. He was back in the outfield; he'd stopped running in when he saw I was about to take it. The player who had said, "I've got it," was some joker in the home team's bullpen. And the ball dropped to the ground.

As an infielder, you shouldn't assume at any time that the outfielder will catch a short fly. One time the right fielder, second baseman, and I converged on a spot where a shallow pop was dropping in short right field. The right fielder thought the second baseman was going to take it and stopped running, and the second baseman, who'd lost sight of the ball for a moment, couldn't get to it. I dived and was lucky to make the catch. But luck wouldn't have done the trick if I'd seen the ball heading toward right field and had decided someone over there would take it.

Wherever the ball is popped, particularly on a glary day, you may be the only player with the right angle of sight to make the catch. So, until someone else calls for it or calls you off, go after it. You've got nothing else to do with your time while the pop is hanging up there. And the heads-up player who goes after everything is the one who often wins ball games for his team.

Sun and occasionally lights add to the difficulty of catching a pop-up. We wear sunglasses, but sometimes they aren't good enough and we have to shield our eyes with our glove. I'm constantly testing to determine whether the sun is going to pose a problem. It's a good idea during the infield practice between innings to look up and see whether you're going to have to rely on your glasses. If you're not prepared and you lose sight of the ball, sometimes just for an instant, you won't be able to make the catch.

When a ball is popped up and the sun or glare is strong enough to give trouble, I flip my glasses down right away. There have been times when I've flipped them and couldn't see the sky, so I just reached up and grabbed my hat and tossed everything away, the way a catcher would with his mask. Few big-leaguers have the ability to turn their backs on a pop-up, go where they think it's headed, turn around, and find it coming down right there. Most players have to keep looking right up at the ball. So glasses are valuable, and, if your team can afford good ones, use them. Make sure they're not breakable, because that's dangerous. A couple of times I've dived for a ball and hit right on the glasses, and I have scars to show where the frame dug into the side of my face. If the glasses had been breakable, it really would have spelled trouble.

If your club can't afford to buy good glasses that don't break, then learn to shade your eyes with your glove or bare hand, depending on which side the sun is at. Bob Aspromonte never uses glasses; he prefers to shade. But—maybe you've heard this before—it takes practice.

CATCHING THE BATTED BALL

You've sighted the pop fly, you've judged it correctly, you've got plenty of time. Now, how do you catch it? Many players catch a ball down low, but I don't recommend that. Just as with fielding a ground ball, I like to have my glove and other hand up where I can see them. It's much easier to judge the ball that way. Also, when your hands are above your head, there's more catching surface, and it's easier to close your glove that way than when your arms are in an awkward position.

Thousands of young ballplayers idolize Willie Mays,

and because his style is the basket catch, they want to catch fly balls the same way. But there's no sense in doing that, because Willie's style may not be best for you. I've used a basket catch, which is difficult for me, only when I've misjudged a ball or when I'm going out in the outfield to catch one over my head. Even if you should find in later years that a basket catch is for you, learn the proper, safer way now.

Basket style or not, if you try to catch a ball waist-high and it pops out of your glove, you have very little chance of recovering it before it hits the ground. But if you try to catch it over your head and it pops out, you still have a good chance at nabbing it waist-high.

There are major-leaguers who invariably catch one-handed. It looks spectacular, but I think it's taking an unnecessary chance. Unless you're diving or lunging for a ball that can be caught only one-handed, use *two* hands. That way, you have a better feel of the ball, and less chance of dropping it.

To summarize: Get under a pop fly when it's at the top of its arc, so you feel as if it's going to hit you on the head. Be sure to call for a pop or signal that you have it. If you know you can't take it, help out by calling to your teammate that he should take it. If an outfielder and you, the infielder, have an equal chance at catching a pop, let him take it. But don't assume anyone else is going to catch it. Go after everything until a teammate calls you off.

If your team can afford them, wear sunglasses in the

field, but only unbreakable ones. Check the sun before the game and between innings. Whether or not you wear glasses, learn to shade your eyes with your hand.

Catch a pop fly over the level of your head—and use two hands.

THROWING: NO LOLLIPOPS, PLEASE

Say there's a runner on first and one out, and the ball is grounded sharply to you—an ideal double-play set-up. How hard do you throw it? Well, I try to have something on the ball, because the second baseman is going to be coming over at pretty good speed and he's going to have to change his rhythm if it's underthrown. Besides, it's easier for him to get it away if it's over-thrown.

I know when I'm covering second on a double-play ball, a lot of times I get into trouble if the second base-man throws it to me too softly. If he "lollipops" it, as we say, if he lobs the ball, I've got to change gears, slow down to catch it, and be more deliberate in throwing it on to first. These extra moments can mean the batter is going to be safe at first. The faster the ball gets to the pivot man, the better chance he has of completing the double play, even if he's a bit slow in getting rid of the ball.

In throwing to any base, especially to second on a double-play ball, "letter-high" is the recommended target for the throw. The reason is that that's the level your eyes naturally take in at a glance. Also, the pivot man coming to the bag is likely to have his hands and glove up around his letters, ready to take the ball and gun it on to first. It's a lot easier for him to catch it at that level than knee-high, especially if it's thrown hard. Throw it to him low and you really change his rhythm, because then he's actually defensing to catch the ball. He'll be off stride in his effort to catch it, and there'll be little chance you'll get the double play.

I just try to throw the ball firmly. If I've got time, I straighten up a little bit and throw from the top. If there isn't time, I just throw it from where I get it and hope it's high enough for my d.p. partner to handle comfortably.

It's all a matter of constant practice between the shortstop and second baseman. You shouldn't have to be telling yourself, "Gee, I've got to throw it letter-high." It should become so commonplace and natural that you do it automatically.

Timing, too, is something that develops with practice. Some players have difficulty getting the ball to the pivot man at the right instant. You should try to give it to him just as he's reaching the bag. If you're prepared to throw and he's not there, throw it anyway, because otherwise, if you start to throw and hold back, you won't be able to throw with any authority when you do let go, and your accuracy may be off, too. But the second baseman or shortstop who's covering is

Making the double play. The shortstop should drag his foot across the base as he receives the throw, which should be chest high and in front of him. Keep the ball below the glove and hop out of the baseline. Take a step away from the bag, pivot (turn) your hips, and throw to first base.

usually within range, and will get there on time to receive the throw.

When you're the pivot man on a double play, the first thing you do is make the play and worry about the runner sliding in later. In other words, you make the putout and the throw on to first almost as if the runner wasn't there. You don't just stand there and let him slide into you—that wouldn't be smart—but nine times out of ten I never even look at the man sliding in because I'm watching the second baseman, taking the throw from him on the run, and turning to throw to our first baseman. If you have your hands out in front of you to take the throw, as you should, you can see both the ball coming and the runner, without actually looking at him. You'll get out of the way as a reflex action. If you worry about him, it will affect your consistency.

Contrary to popular opinion, runners don't come in with spikes high, to break up a double play. Every runner comes in trying to take you out of the play, but without injuring you. They might brush you with their shin, for example. I've had players come and accidentally spike me or knock me down, but then they'll help me up and ask if I'm okay. Since I'm not the type of ballplayer who goes after anyone else, nobody is really after me.

One point to keep in mind in the pivot: after you reach for the ball, drag your foot across the bag. This way, you don't have to search for the bag and there's less margin for error. Also, it's better than trying to plant your foot on top of the bag, because if you step on the bag wrong you could stumble or even sprain or break your ankle. The pivot isn't done the same way all the time, but in general it's better to do it this way.

To summarize: The double play needs precision teamwork between the shortstop and second baseman. As one fields the ball, the other breaks for the bag. If you're the player taking the grounder, you throw the ball to your teammate letter-high and put some "oomph" into it. You try to time your throw so that the ball reaches your partner just as he's getting to the bag.

You make the best throw you can, depending on how much time you have.

The pivot man, meanwhile, hurries over to the bag, hands in front of him, around the letters, to take his partner's throw. He just about ignores the runner sliding in, depending on reflex action to get out of the runner's way. The pivot man drags his foot across the bag to make the force-out, then whips the ball to first base for the double play.

THE SHORTSTOP AND THE PITCHER

A shortstop has a bird's-eye view of his pitcher. He can tell whether the hurler is throwing the ball too hard, or not hard enough, or whether he's falling off the mound. The pitching coach can't keep coming out to talk to the hurler—if he comes out more than twice, he must change pitchers—and it puts pressure on the pitcher when the coach comes out. So I talk to our pitcher quite a bit, often trivia, but enough to steady him or change his thinking.

Danny Frisella was once throwing very cautiously to a slugger in a tight situation. He was being too careful, so I told him: "That guy's just like you and me— [except for batting average, home runs, and RBIs]— throw it." He did, and he retired him.

If a pitcher's thrown six balls in a row, apparently he's not thinking properly. Maybe he's not concentrating, or his motion and timing are bad. If you can get him to think about something, it may not be what's wrong, but if, say, you tell him, "You're rushing," he may not be rushing but he'll change his thinking.

Gary Gentry had walked one batter and had a 2–0 count on the next. I told him: "I only see your number 39 in front of me." He understood that what I meant was he hadn't been bending over, following through on his pitches the way he should have been. It started him thinking, and he made the correction and regained his control.

Every pitcher is different. For instance, Tom Seaver is quick to analyze himself and figure out what needs correction. Other pitchers won't listen to advice, and often don't figure out their problems in a given inning or game.

A good bit of strategic thinking is done at a mound conference. Gil Hodges might say, "Fregosi, get in a little more on this—he's going to bunt," or "We've got first base open. You don't have to throw this man a strike—I don't care if you walk him." Or he might ask, "Would you rather walk him or pitch to him?" or "Do you feel all right?" or "Try to keep the ball down in this situation—we'll get two." Comments of this type often have the value of instilling a little confidence in the pitcher, even if it's just a matter of saying something the pitcher already knows.

Sometimes a mound conference is used to stall for time while a reliever warms up in the bullpen. Then it's all small talk. The pitcher knows he's coming out, but we try to kill some time. I'll get in front of the pitcher, with my back to the umpire, and say, "Let me know when he starts this way and I'll leave." When the pitcher tells me the umpire is coming, I go.

DROPPING THE BALL—ON PURPOSE

Some young players try to be cute and deliberately drop a ball in order to force a man or turn a one-out play into a double play. I don't recommend it. For one thing, there's the infield fly rule, and a similar rule about dropping a line drive intentionally. Then, there's the danger that the ball you let drop will bounce away from you—and you end up behind the eight ball.

Some people were on me in the 1969 World Series for not trying a dropped-ball trick. Paul Blair of the Orioles was on first and somebody hit a pop fly. These critics thought I should have dropped it and tried for a force-out and possible double play, but I caught it. (Some of them may have arrived at their decision after it turned out that Blair stole second base and eventually scored.)

But even though I think it's fine during the season to try trick plays and run the risk of losing a game because the tricks don't work out, it's quite another thing to lose a World Series game that way. The fans would have run me out of town. Had I let the ball drop, it would have hit on dirt (we weren't playing on Astroturf) and maybe bounced twenty-five feet in the air, if I didn't smother it. Or I might have kicked it away. With Blair moving, who knows what might have happened?

RELAYS AND CUTOFFS

As a shortstop, you play an important part in throws from the outfield to the infield on a base hit. You're part of a relay team that can cut down runs and save you ball games, if you execute it correctly.

It's imperative to arrange in your own mind, *before* the play, where you and particular teammates go when the ball is hit to a certain spot. Also, you have to know ahead of time where you're going to throw the ball on

63

the relay, and what base has to be covered. You should have all the possibilities clearly set in your mind.

Let's say a ball is hit to right-center field for a sure double and possible triple, so there's no point to covering second base. The second baseman would go out to take the throw from the outfielder and I'd line up about twenty or twenty-five feet behind the second baseman, in case the throw goes over or under him. This is called a double cutoff, since two men are involved in the middle of the relay. Whichever of us gets the ball would relay it on to third. To hold the runner at second or get him at third requires perfect execution all along.

How far an infielder goes out on a relay depends on how good his arm is and how good the outfielder's arm is. I may go out farther than another infielder because I have a strong arm and it's easier for the outfielder to make a relatively short throw to me, and then have me make the longer throw from the outfield. With a strong-armed outfielder like Tommie Agee, you don't have to go out quite so far.

The important things to remember: First of all, line yourself up with the base that the throw is likely to be coming to. Secondly, make sure you hold your arms up so the outfielder has something to sight on.

It takes practice until you can automatically line yourself up between the outfielder and the bag—say, second base—on a hit that is not a sure double. Until you get the feel of where you are in relation to the

When taking a relay throw from the out-field, keep your arms up so the fielder can use you as a target. Your full body should face the fielder but your left foot should be slightly back, making it easier to turn and throw.

base you want to line up with, run out and turn side-ways to check the angle you're at. Then adjust so you're in a straight line between fielder and base and get your hands up. Be ready to take the throw and pivot almost in the same motion.

Getting your hands up is so important, and yet young players often forget to do it. If the outfielder who's retrieved the ball has to wheel around, he can easily lose his sense of direction in a big ball park un-less he's got something to sight on.

As a cutoff man, it's up to you whether to let the

ball through to the base, cut it off and hold it, or throw to a different base. It's one of the most difficult decisions to make in a game.

Suppose there are men on first and second and the batter hits a shallow single to left field. The fielder is going to try to throw the lead runner out at the plate. Should the cutoff man (on this play the third baseman; the shortstop would cover third) let the throw go through? Or would he be better off to intercept and try to keep the runner on first from going to third? He'd have to take a number of factors into consideration and then make up his mind in a split second. He'd have to watch how much time the play had consumed and how much of a jump the runner had got from second; if there were less than two outs, on a high line drive the runner would have had to hold up to see if it was caught. Then the cutoff man would have to see what kind of jump the outfielder had on the ball. Positioned as he is in the infield—on a shallow hit, the cutoff man sees everything that matters—he can see third base to his left and second base to his right. If he sees that the throw is coming in on a line and the runner from second has just hit third base, he's likely to let it through. But if the runner had passed long before the throw came in, he's likely to cut it off. And if the throw is off line, he's got to cut it off to keep the runner from first making it to third.

In the seventh game of the 1971 World Series, Willie Stargell bounced a single to left to open the eighth

66

inning for the Pirates, and Jose Pagan laced a double to deep center field. Merv Rettenmund, the Orioles' center fielder, who said he tried to throw it before he had it, bobbled the ball a little before getting off a strong throw to Mark Belanger, the shortstop, who was the relay man. Belanger gunned it home, but first baseman Boog Powell cut the ball off about eight feet in front of the plate. I thought Boog had no reason to cut it off, since there was no chance of getting Pagan at second, but Powell said afterwards, "We didn't have a chance to get Stargell" at home, and catcher Elrod Hendricks agreed with Boog's assessment of the situation.

The cutoff man does get help, especially from the catcher, who has the whole play in front of him. The catcher will yell, "Cut," or "Cut third," if he thinks the ball is off line or late and should be intercepted and thrown to third to cut down the man there.

ANTI-STEALING

Sometimes a burglary takes place because the home-owner or storekeeper didn't do enough to prevent it—didn't lock all the doors or make sure mail and newspapers didn't pile up. Well, sometimes bases get stolen in baseball because the defending team didn't do enough to prevent it.

By and large, you don't steal bases off the catcher. There are some receivers with bad arms or some who

67

don't throw, but they don't generally last in the majors too long. You steal on the pitcher. It's up to him to make sure that a runner doesn't get a good jump, and to throw over to the base or look over often enough to make him hesitant about taking a big lead. But the infielder can't defense against it at all. You just hope that, if the runner goes, the catcher makes a good throw. If he's called for a pitchout, he's got a better chance of getting the runner, even with a quick getaway, since the catcher will be stepping out to get the ball and be able to get it away quicker. Otherwise, the catcher just has to wait for the pitch to come in. The second baseman or shortstop doesn't go over to cover the bag until he sees the runner break.

SAY "AH": COVERING ON A STEAL OR HIT-AND-RUN

Because I play every day and know the signals each pitcher uses, I know every pitch coming. So of course I know when a pitchout is coming, simply by watching the catcher. It's up to me to tell the second baseman which of us is covering on the steal attempt. I tell him by putting my glove in front of my face and either opening my mouth and sort of saying "ah" to indicate he should cover, or closing my mouth and saying "mm," telling him that I'll cover.

Whether it's a steal attempt or a sure hit-and-run

try (often the two go together), deciding who will cover the base is like deciding where to play a man: you have to know the hitter. If he's a right-handed hitter who is a good hit-and-run man, I might take a chance and cover second, because we know he's going to be trying to hit behind the runner. With most left-handed hitters I almost always cover, because, if it's hit-and-run and he goes to the opposite field, it's no big setback. The left fielder is in a lot better position to hold the lead runner from scoring than the right fielder. In a sense, then, by my covering second we're encouraging the left-handed hitter to try to punch to left.

Some hitters pose special problems because of their great abilities. When Matty Alou is up, for example, I generally wait until the last possible instant to cover second because, if it's a hit-and-run play, Matty will hit the ball even if the pitch is over his head or into the dirt. But if it's a pitchout, I break immediately, because even a Matty Alou can't hit a pitchout.

TIME AND DAYLIGHT: PICK-OFF PLAYS

When you think a man is going to steal, that's a good time to try to pick him off. When you know a man just *has* to steal a base, that's the *best* time to try to pick him off.

There are two basic kinds of pick-off plays: time and daylight.

69

For the time play, I give a sign to the catcher and he gives it to the pitcher, disguising it with a sign for a regular pitch. The reason for the disguise is that the man on second can see the catcher's fingers, and you don't want to arouse his suspicions. There are different ways the catcher then shows the pitcher which man is covering. Both shortstop and second baseman might have signaled for a pick-off at the same time, so he touches his left leg to show it's the shortstop who'll be taking the throw, or his right leg to indicate the second baseman. The pitcher pretends to be taking the sign for a pitch before his stretch. He knows not to do anything until the catcher gives him the key. Then, as the shortstop or second baseman breaks for the bag, the catcher gives the pitcher a sign; the pitcher wheels around and throws, and—if all has gone well—you've got a pick-off.

The Chicago Cubs work a pretty play with a man on second. The shortstop makes an elaborate fake as if a pick-off is in the making, then, with the runner bluffed back to the bag, goes back to his normal position. The runner, feeling secure, wanders off into his lead again, and—whammo!—the second baseman has zipped in behind him, ready for the pitcher's delayed pick-off throw.

We used to use a time play where I'd give the signal, the pitcher would take his stretch, and as soon as I saw the back of his head I'd break, and he'd count "one thousand one, one thousand two," and so on, throwing at a predetermined second. The trouble with that system is that not everyone counts the same.

In a daylight play (so called because the shortstop places daylight between himself and the runner, to signal the pitcher) I tell the pitcher when I'm going to break, and he waits until I get between the runner and the base. For this play he has to be looking at me, so he takes his stretch, looks back and waits for me to beat my man, then steps off the rubber and throws to me. Sometimes it works because the runner is walking casually off the bag, convinced that no one is ready yet. Maybe he's only five feet off—he hasn't taken his lead yet—but he's gawking or not paying attention.

I think you really pick more men off by the daylight method than by a time play, which has to be so precise. Too, the daylight play is actually a lot faster than a time pick-off because often the pitcher hasn't even got a pick-off sign from the catcher; he just happens to have looked back, and you go. And too, in a time play, the pitcher doesn't really see whether you have the man beaten; he just wheels and throws.

When the second baseman is going to cover on a pick-off play, it's my job to back him up. But I don't go toward the bag; I head toward shallow center field. That way, I can get a ball that's deflected that otherwise would have gone into center field. If the throw goes over the second baseman's head on a line, there's no possible way I can get to it, but if it bounces off his glove and goes up in the air softly, I can prevent it from going to the outfield. It works the same way on a steal attempt, except that I've got to wait in my position to make sure the batter misses the ball before going to back up.

It's very difficult to pick men off nowadays. Players who aren't good runners don't usually take a big enough lead to get picked off. Half the time, they aren't going to be able to score on a base hit anyway, so there's no great concern about them. Everyone who takes a big lead is a good runner, and you can very seldom pick him off, except on a trick play or when he's napping.

The best you can do is to try to hold a runner like this close enough to second so he won't score on a hit. One way to do this is to "kick" the runner back by taking a step or two in the direction of the bag as if you're going to try to pick him off. With Hank Aaron, who takes a lead at second and turns around and keeps looking at me, I like to do that all day. I keep kicking as if I'm going to the bag; my hope is he'll take one step back while the pitcher is throwing the ball home. Then, if the batter hits, Hank has to turn around and find out what's happening, and he's delayed in running on a hit.

RUNDOWNS

When you have a man in a rundown, it should be a

sure out, providing you avoid the mistakes that are all too easily made.

First of all, try to make as few throws as possible. If you cut down on the number you make, you cut down the chances of making a bad one. It's important to run the man back to the bag he came from, so that if something goes wrong, and you don't get him out, at least he hasn't advanced.

Often, young players will run at the man, carrying the ball at their side, swinging their arms as they would when running without the ball. I used to do that, and I found it created two problems. First of all, when I decided to throw, I'd first have to bring the ball up to throwing position, and that wasted a precious instant that might have meant the putout. Also, it was difficult to fake a throw, because the runner knew I wasn't going to throw until I brought my arm up. So, keep your arm in throwing position as you run. The man won't know when you're going to throw and when you're faking. And you can let the ball go without hesitation.

Try to get a good angle in the rundown, so that the runner isn't blocking your vision or the path your throw will take. If you're right-handed (and as short-stop or second or third baseman you would be), stay a little bit to the right of the runner so you can throw unimpeded, and so the man you're throwing to can see the ball. If you're lefty (say, as a first baseman), stay on the left side for the same reasons.

73

When you're close enough to tag the runner along the base path, try to tag him low, though not as low as his ankles. A runner caught in a rundown will try to fake you with his head and the top of his body, and get away from you. But the bottom of his body has to go with his legs, so if you aim at the bottom you won't go wrong. He won't be able to fake you or suddenly sit down or slide to avoid a high tag.

There's a coverage pattern that infielders will use on a rundown. Say we've got a man picked off first and the first baseman is running him toward me. I like to run up, because standing back would give the man the opportunity to do a lot of "dances" in between. The first baseman should run him toward me, then give me the ball. I will run the man toward first, without letting him get back to first. Meanwhile, the second baseman will come over and cover second, and the pitcher should go to first. (If the second baseman had been involved in the action, I'd go in and cover behind him.) If it's done right, it should take only one throw. When I get the throw I'm going to be running at the man with enough momentum to catch him.

Reviewing some of the things to remember about a rundown: Keep throws to a minimum to avoid chance of error. Run the man toward the bag he came from, and, when you have the ball, keep your arm in throwing position so there's no delay in getting the ball away and so you can more easily fake a throw. Stay to your throwing side of the runner, so he doesn't block the throw and so your teammate can see the ball. Tag the runner low. Make sure you know your coverage position: if the shortstop and first baseman are conducting the rundown, the second baseman should cover second and the pitcher, first base.

THE TAG

Many young ballplayers get in trouble when they try to tag the runner coming to a base because they swipe at him with the ball up in the air instead of tagging the bag—that is, holding the ball in front of the bag, where the runner has to come. If you don't hold it in front of the bag, it's too easy to be faked out by the runner. You reach out to tag him, but he slides to the side and avoids you altogether. Or you try to tag him on the chest or hip, and he manages to touch the bag with his foot before you touch him with the ball.

No matter what kind of slide he uses, he's got to come to the base, so when I get the ball in my glove I come right down with it in front of the bag. If I see his foot is going to the side, it's an easy matter just to move the ball in that direction.

ERRORS

I talked before about the most difficult thing for a shortstop to do; now, here's the easiest. The easiest

75

Here is how you receive the throw from the catcher on a steal. ABOVE RIGHT: *the proper way to make the tag, letting the runner slide into the tag.* BELOW: *the wrong way to attempt a tag, going after the runner. Here you are committed, and it is easy for the base runner to hook ground your tag.*

thing in the world for any ballplayer is to make an error.

That's because there is so much involved in a play. You have to get the proper jump on the ball, you have to make sure the ball doesn't play you, you have to field the ball and get it out of your glove cleanly, and you have to make an accurate throw. Do one of these things wrong and you've made an error.

The basic cause of errors is lack of concentration. Consequently, you're not aggressive enough; you're too lax and you let the ball play you a little bit.

Throwing errors often come from hurrying your throw. Sometimes that can't be avoided, but there are times when you find yourself throwing from an awkward position when you really had time to set yourself in a better position and make a better throw. An example of that would be when a batter who's a slow runner hits one into the hole. You backhand the ball and throw it underhand, although actually, because of the man's slowness, there is enough time for you to circle around and throw it three-quarters.

An error isn't always the fielder's fault. Sometimes field conditions play a part. A ball will bounce differently on wet ground than on dry or artificial turf. It may come up six inches higher than you expected because the ground is hard, or stay down because the ground is wet. Those are really judgment errors. In a game in the summer of 1971, played after a couple of days of rain, I tried to stop a ball, but my right foot hit the grass and I skidded about three feet. Even though my footing was gone, though, there was still a chance to get the ball, which was right underneath me—but I missed it entirely.

On another play that same game, I backhanded a ball and tried to stop, but skidded. I started to fall backwards, but I threw anyway. In that case the scorer credited the man with a base hit.

I think pressure contributes to errors. Say there's a man on third, the potential winning run, in the bottom of the ninth. Two are out and a tough grounder is hit to you. Make the putout and your team is still alive in extra innings. Fail to make it and you've lost the game. It's hard to tell yourself, "Relax," in circumstances like that. And so, instead of being your old relaxed self, you tense up, and then you're not fluid. The ball might hit you right in the glove—this has happened to me— and, because you're tense, it's as if you had a piece of steel on your hands. You kind of jab at the ball and knock it right back out of your glove.

On the other hand, you can be relaxed when you shouldn't be. Aggressive fielders get charged for errors on balls that others don't even try for. And there are infielders who don't charge the ball very hard when they should; they take their time, field the ball cleanly, and make a throw that the man beats out. But the fielder can't be charged with an error; it's credited as a base hit. On the same kind of ball, though, an aggressive fielder will charge it as hard as he possibly can and try to scoop it up with one hand. If he's successful, he can throw the batter out by twenty feet, whereas if he waited, he would have no chance to get him. So the man who charges in and hustles gets an error, while the lazier man doesn't.

In 1970, I was lucky enough to tie a major league record for most consecutive games—54—without an error for shortstop.* Certainly, I'm proud of that. But better proof that I was having a good season are my figures for putouts (305, which led the league) and assists (401).

I'd rather be the aggressive type of fielder. I may make more errors than a lackadaisical fielder, but I'll get more putouts and assists than he will, and help the team by getting to every ball I possibly can.

* Two other men in the Mets' 1971 infield held records for the National League for consecutive errorless games at their position—Bob Aspromonte, third baseman (57), and Ken Boswell, second baseman (85).

3. At Bat

BASICALLY, THERE ARE two types of hitters —the "naturals" and the "self-mades."

The natural hitter is often one who, the less thinking he does about hitting, the better off he is. Hank Aaron is that type. If he ever broke down how he hit, he'd be in trouble, because he goes against some of the rules of hitting. Willie Mays is another basic, natural hitter. They scare you just by walking up to the plate. On the other side, you have fellows like Matty Alou. He struggled and struggled for a few years, and then he won a batting title because he made himself a good hitter. He learned something that I try to keep in mind: you can't be something that you're not. Although he was small, he used to try to hit for distance. That didn't work. Then he decided to become a contact hitter, a man you can't strike out, a player who hits 90 percent of the balls either on the ground or as line drives, and very few fly balls. Now he's essentially a singles hitter, but he gets 200 of them, to equal the output of a long-ball hitter in value to his club. Nelson Fox was another example of a player who made himself into a good hitter. He couldn't run, but he learned to hit.

When you start out it's best just to play and not try to pattern yourself after anyone, because you're likely to change with time and experience. Many youngsters idolize players and want to be like them too soon. You can idolize a major-league star and want to be like him, but, let's face it—you can't be like him when you're nine years old.

You can't even be like some of the older kids you play with. I'll give you an example. When I was in Little League, there were some twelve-year-olds who were six-one and six-two and could hit the ball a mile. Put them in a park with a big-league fence and once in a while they'd be able to knock it over. I wanted to be able to hit like they did. But even though I hit the ball pretty well for my size, I couldn't match their power. Still, it took me until the minor leagues to analyze myself and face the facts. I was hitting .220, popping a lot of balls in the air. This woke me up. I realized that if I was ever going to make a living out of baseball, play the game professionally, I'd have to do something consistently. Either be a slugger—which I couldn't be—or get on base by being hit like Ron

Hunt, or by having a good eye and being a contact hitter.

What it amounts to is that you should just take advantage of what God gave you. If He didn't give you the brute strength to hit it over the wall, don't try to hit it over the wall.

You've heard this before, but it bears repeating: Don't try to be what you're not.

DEVELOPING STRENGTH

Whatever your build, there are ways you can develop your strength as a batter.

There are major-leaguers like Gil Hodges, who is not especially muscular but has a very wide back. His strength is geared from the shoulders up. Then there are players like Art Shamsky who is light for his height. Art is strong from the wrists to the shoulders, what we call a forearm or wrist hitter. He's the Henry Aaron or Ernie Banks type, not very muscular, but blessed with very quick wrists. Players like this don't require a long swing to get power. They can take a short swing, but their wrist action is firm and they really smack the ball.

If you want to develop your wrists and arms, there are machines that you can buy, or you can create your own apparatus. A few years back I bought a golf exerciser with two little barbells and a weight with a handle on the end of the rope. But I've also used home-made devices. One was a rope tied on a stick with a ten-pound weight at the bottom of it. I'd roll it up with my wrists and then roll it down. Your arms get very tired very quickly, but you can almost feel the strength building in your wrists, hands, and forearms. It's important to have strength there because of the part they play, not only in hitting, but in throwing and pitching.

You can accomplish the same thing with an ordinary towel. Double the towel up into a wad. Then, with your wrists working in opposite directions, twist it one way, then another, and keep at it.

If you're interested enough in improving, you can put your imagination to work and, with a little initiative, build all sorts of things on your own to help yourself as a hitter. You can rig up a sort of high tee from which you practice hitting. You can put a hole through a ball, attach it by rope to a pole in the ground or to a tree—and swing away.

LEFT, RIGHT, OR SWITCH?

Many boys watch switch-hitters, myself included, and wonder if they shouldn't do the same. Their fathers will say to me, "My son is fast and small like you. Shouldn't he switch-hit?" My answer is, "Definitely not." Why? Because he's playing only once or twice a week. I know from experience that you can become good at anything only by repetition. If you're playing infrequently, you might as well concentrate on hitting one way. You might start out on your first at-bat in a game not feeling comfortable, but you adjust on subsequent turns at the plate. But if, say, the opposing team started with a right-handed pitcher and you hit lefty, and then they bring in a southpaw and you swing righty, you don't get a chance to adjust.

I play every day and I know the way I'm hitting the most—say, left-handed—is the way I'm hitting the best.

Incidentally, until 1966 I hit only right-handed. I didn't become a switch-hitter until well into my career. (Maury Wills, an inspiration to all ballplayers my size, gave me a lot of incentive to make the move. If he hadn't switch-hit, he might not have made it as a major-leaguer.) And I don't recommend that any young ballplayer try to become one until at least high school, where there are the facilities, the time to learn, the people to teach you, and the opportunity to practice and practice. Why suffer, trying to hit both ways, when you can concentrate on the way you find more natural—and have fun at the game? At age nine or ten, don't try to mold yourself into a major-leaguer. If it's frustrating for me at twenty-seven, it's surely going to be for you at your age. Fathers and coaches shouldn't try to make big-leaguers out of their boys.

Baseball is a natural game, in the sense that when

you first start you throw the way that's most comfortable and you hit the way that's most comfortable. So your decision on which side of the plate to swing from should be based on what's most comfortable. True, there are boys who feel equally comfortable batting righty or lefty. But if they want to become switch-hitters, I still recommend that they wait at least until high school. Pick out the way you're a better hitter and stick with that in the game, but when you're playing pepper on the sidelines or stickball in the street, hit from the other side, so you've got something extra to fall back on in the future. (In one Little League game when I was nine, I did hit left-handed, but that was because we were winning 10–0, and our manager, my dad, said, "Everybody hits left-handed," just to break the monotony.)

I'm able to throw left-handed, too, though not as well as right-handed, because I used to throw rocks lefty just to learn how.

There are advantages and disadvantages to hitting from either side of the plate. A left-handed hitter is generally platooned more often than a right-handed batsman, because since the beginning of time there have been more right-handed pitchers, so righty batters are more accustomed to facing righty hurlers than left-handed batters are to facing southpaws. On our team, Ken Boswell and Ed Kranepool, left-handed hitters, are substituted for when the opposition brings in a lefty. But when a righty is going, you don't see right-handed hitters Cleon Jones or Tommie Agee on the bench.

But there are advantages to hitting left-handed. For example, if you're a good runner you don't have to hit the ball as hard to beat out a hit as a right-handed batsman does. If you slap it, the ball goes to the shortstop and he's got a long throw to make, whereas if a righty waits on a pitch and slaps it, it goes to the second baseman, who's got only a short twenty-foot throw to make.

FACING THE PITCH

Standing up at the plate, just sixty and a half feet away from a fellow who is going to send a hardball hurtling toward you at speeds up to a hundred miles an hour, you've got some cause for concern. In 1963 in the minors, after five weeks of professional ball, I was hit by a pitch that broke my left arm. Then in 1965 Jack Hamilton, who joined the Mets the following year, hit me with a pitch and broke two ribs.

But you can't take a pessimistic view about being hit and still expect to be a good, aggressive hitter.

It's like being the pivot man on a double play. If I worried about the man coming into me—Wayne Graham once took me out with such gusto I needed a knee operation—I'd never make the double play. By the same token, if every one of the six hundred or so times I walked up to the plate in a season, I said to myself,

86

"This guy might hit me in the head with the ball and then it will be all over for me," I'd never be able to hit the ball.

So, like being taken out at second base, you've just got to get up and brush yourself off. It's part of the game. Of something like 1,800 pitches you're going to see in a season, one of them is going to hit you; one of them is going to be wild and you won't be able to get out of the way in time. But if you're going to worry about it, it's going to affect your aggressiveness and your chances of success as a hitter.

So, unless you're deliberately trying to change your stride to hit to the opposite field, go into the ball. Heaven protects the aggressive hitter.

SIZE AND POWER

You have to be strong to be a power hitter, but size has little to do with it. Some of the better power hitters are not particularly tall and don't weigh very much. Jim Wynn of the Houston Astros is a good example. At five-nine and 165 pounds, he looks like a small package of dynamite—and one season he exploded for thirty-seven homers.

PICKING A BAT

A big, heavy bat isn't going to turn you into a big, heavy hitter. In fact, it may put an extra burden on your hitting because, while it's capable of giving the ball a good ride, you're probably not capable of managing it.

The bat you use should be comfortable—like the glove you wear in the field—something you can control for a solid swing. I like a relatively thick-handled bat, but some players can't stand one like that. There are heavy bats with thin handles with the weight concentrated on the end; light bats with thick handles, and all sorts of combinations. Pick one that your size hands can hold comfortably and one you can swing with relative ease.

GRIPPING THE BAT

Basically, there are three kinds of grips on a bat. In the full-length grip, the hitter has his hands all the way down at the end of the handle, down near the knob. This is usually the way the distance-hitters hold on. In the second grip, the modified full-length, the hands are an inch or two higher on the bat, for better control combined with power. The third is the choke-up, in which the hands are well up on the bat handle for maximum control.

I've always choked up because I never felt comfortable down at the end of the bat. Never having been particularly strong physically, I find the bat doesn't feel as heavy when I choke up; it's a little more bal-

This is the bat position for a contact or singles hitter. Your grip is up from the knob, hands close to the body. You are trying to slap at the ball.

This is the position favored by long-ball or power hitters. The bat is farther back and away from the body, the grip down near the knob of the bat.

anced. And you have a lot easier time making contact when you're choked. Of course, that kind of grip takes away inches of hitting power, and thus you're sacrificing distance. But I find it most comfortable. You should find what's most comfortable for you.

Except for a couple of individual stylists who leave a little space on the bat between their hands, most players grasp the bat with the side of the index finger of their bottom hand (the left one, if you're hitting righty) touching the side of the pinkie of their top hand. (There have been players who interlocked those fingers.) The second knuckles of the top hand are usually lined up somewhere between the base knuckles and second knuckles of the bottom hand. The thumbs are around the handle.

THE BATTER'S BOX

Comfort again is a key in deciding where you should stand in the batter's box—up front or back, close to the plate or away from it. You should be close enough to make contact with balls over the outside of the plate. Batters who like to pull stand close to the plate. Those who hit straight away stand about a foot away.

When I hit right-handed, I like to crowd the plate because I'm a pull hitter from that side. I want to crowd it so they'll throw me inside, which is where I like to get the ball.

When I hit left-handed I like the ball away, so I can hit to the opposite field. I hit better to the left because I'm not a wrist hitter. I like the ball away from me so I can stride into it. If I fell away from the plate, I wouldn't be able to reach a pitch that came right over.

As a general rule, most hitters prefer an inside pitch. Overall, it's the easiest pitch to hit solidly because you're out in front with your bat. But I like the ball away. For one thing, I'm not that strong, batting left-handed, and an outside pitch takes less effort to hit. I don't have to be very fast and get my bat way out. A ball that's away is one you can hit late and just loft to left or right field.

But a breaking pitch away—in particular a slider, which is really a flat curve—can be the most difficult pitch in the world. You're prepared for it to come inside or over, and you open your hips and bring your bat around to meet the ball. But the ball breaks away, and you've got to lunge at it awkwardly. If you do connect, you don't hit it with any authority. As a right-hander, I found the only way I could deal with that kind of ball was to look for the outside pitch and just make contact with it.

Two men may have equal strength, but one man is faster with the bat, and that will help determine where he stands in the batter's box. Early in the season I may start out even with the plate, and then later in the season go back—sometimes with my back foot on the back line of the box—because that gives an extra fraction of a second to meet the ball. It all depends on how fast I am with my bat.

Bat speed will also dictate in part how close a man stands to the plate. The fellow who's slower with the bat isn't going to look for pitches inside; he's going to wait for pitches away because he can be a little bit later on the ball when it's out there. Ken Singleton's strength is out there, so they pitch him in; Shamsky's strength is on a pitch that's in—where you can't be late if you want to hit that ball out in front. So the pitchers are smart enough to pitch him on the outside.

THE STRIDE

The step that's taken with your front foot as the pitch comes in is called the *stride*. It may be taken toward or away from the plate, depending on the speed and location of the pitch.

Sometimes—say, with two strikes on you—you may not use any stride at all. If you want to hit to the opposite field on an inside pitch, you'll move your feet. But most times you'll be striding into the pitch. How much of a stride varies with the individual. It should be long enough to give you momentum, direction, and power, but not so long that it costs you balance. Mel Ott, a left-handed hitter, used to raise his right foot as he strode to meet the ball. It looked awkward, but it helped him get leverage and he was comfortable with it. Luckily, his manager, John McGraw, didn't try to change him, and Ott became one of the leading home-run hitters of all time. But he was one in a million; I wouldn't recommend foot raising for anyone else.

STANCE AND SWING

Batters stand different ways at the plate—for comfort and efficiency as hitters. The two things go together. In different circumstances, though, the same batter will use different stances.

There are three fundamental stances: the parallel stance, in which both feet are about the same distance from the plate; the closed stance, in which the front foot is closer to the plate than the back foot, and the open stance, in which the front foot is farther away from the plate than the back foot. It's probably best to start with the parallel stance and gradually find your own best location.

I generally use a closed stance because, especially batting left-handed, I want to be covering the plate at all times. If I were away from the plate, I'd be wrong to use an open stance when, on an outside pitch, I'd either have to come back close or stay open and not be able to reach the ball.

With a man on first I want a ball in, so I can hit it to right field. Therefore, I'll crowd the plate. But if I just want to get on base, I'll use the closed stance without

Normal stance. Also known as "box" or "square." Both feet are an equal distance from the plate.

Closer stance. The front foot is closer to plate.

Open stance. The front foot is farther away from plate.

Here I use a normal stance, back from the plate. My knees are slightly bent and I'm bending over from the waist.

crowding the plate. And, with two strikes on me, I'm likely to go to a more open stance, still close to the plate.

What stance should *you* use? It depends on what's comfortable, after a process of trial and error. Every hitter wants to look like Willie Mays, but what's good for Willie is not necessarily good for you. You've got to try one stance—and give it a good, long trial, even if it doesn't feel good at first. Then, if it still doesn't seem comfortable, try a different one.

As you stand waiting for the pitch, your feet should be comfortably apart, your knees relaxed, hips square with the plate and parallel with your feet. Your arms should be away from your body, so they can swing easily. You'll probably want to keep the forearm of the arm that's facing the pitcher almost parallel to the ground. Your back arm, which supplies the power, can bend some, so that the elbow is toward the ground. The bat should be off the shoulder, ready to be swung in a flat, level arc. Your hands are probably up around the back shoulder.

As the pitcher releases the ball, your weight should shift to the back foot, while the front foot strides smoothly to meet the ball. At the same time, your hips, shoulders, and arms pivot backwards, bringing the bat back with them. To get this coiled power moving forward, you push off the inside of your back foot and begin pivoting forward. Your weight is now all on the front foot, and your hands are in front of your body,

Swing in progress.

with the bat following.

To make contact with the ball (slightly in front of the plate) your wrists snap the bat into contact with the ball. Your back hip swings around at the same time. Then the wrists roll over as you follow through, continuing your swing. And all the while, from delivery to contact, your gaze was intently on the ball and your head was held steady. No jerking it away from the ball.

There are no firm rules about crouching as you await a pitch, or how much to crouch. It's all part of being comfortable. Some players bend from the knees. Others keep their legs straight and bend from the waist over the plate. Still others put their rear ends way out. I find that when I crouch too much I end up actually standing up to hit, and my line of vision has changed. So I'm better off just bending from my waist.

No two individuals are made up alike, have the exact same strength or coordination or speed or eyesight. On four different major-league clubs, you may find that every single one of the hundred ballplayers looks different and swings differently. That's because they haven't patterned themselves after anybody, but have done whatever feels natural for them.

It can't be said too often: Everyone is different. Everyone sees the ball in a different way. The ways men stand at the plate and hold their bats vary tremendously.

But regardless of what a man looks like when he

stands at the plate, regardless of where he holds the bat, how wide his stance, everyone who hits well does basically the same things. In other words, he adheres to the basic fundamentals, such as watching the ball, standing comfortably, using a bat he can handle and holding it so he can control it, then pivoting his body and snapping his wrists as he makes contact with the ball.

No one can just stand with what we ballplayers call "dead hands," stride into that ball, push at it, and expect good results. There has to be some type of bat movement in your hands as you address the ball. Even if it's a Bobby Tolan starting with the bat high above his head, you'll see that, as the ball is coming in, he'll lower the bat and move it backwards to get that bat speed. Just as a pool player moves his cue stick back before he shoots, you've got to have a kind of back-lash motion with a bat to help you propel the ball. There are players with upswings and players who swing down. But basically they all have the bat on the move as they stride to meet the ball.

Wherever you start your stride, whatever your stance or initial bat position, you always have to have some type of movement backwards. Study yourself and find what feels natural for you and allows you to swing through with a fair degree of speed.

To help you see whether there are things about your stance, stride, or swing that need improving, a full-length mirror is a good thing to have. It's always good

The white box shows the strike zone. It extends from the inside and outside corners of the plate, up to just below the shoulders and down to the knees.

to see yourself in "action" and to evaluate your performance honestly to see what you're doing wrong. Are you taking your eye off the ball as it comes in? Are you leaning away as you swing, or striding awkwardly? The mirror will tell you. It will also show you your strike zone.

One word of caution: When using a mirror, keep more than a bat's length away or you'll have seven years' bad luck, starting with having to pick up pieces of shattered glass.

WAIT AND POP

You've probably got about 1/100th of a second to make up your mind about whether or not to swing at a ball. For one thing, the ball gets there so fast. For

99

another, unless you're guessing what pitch is coming or whether it's in or out, you really have to wait to see where the ball is going to be.

Quite a few players go with the motion of the pitcher, striding before the pitch is released, which is why slow pitches are so effective. The batter has committed his body, all his power and his bat, and, unless he happens to be very strong, he has to be content just to push his bat through.

A boy just starting to play baseball seriously can learn from this. Why should you stride or jump, move or start the swing of your bat, when you don't know where the ball is? I think you have to wait until the pitcher releases the ball to find out whether it's in or out, or to know how to stride. If it's in, you're going to have to stride away from the ball, and try to get your hips out and your bat through. But if you've done that and the ball is away, it'll be impossible to reach. It will seem as if the pitch is forty feet away from you.

What I advise is, wait and pop—wait and be quick with your hands and bat. I'll bet if you analyze yourself and look back, you'll remember times when you really didn't move at the plate, but suddenly saw the ball and swung, and hit a solid line drive. It's happened to me. I really didn't see the ball until the last second, but my reactions were right, the basics all came together, and I had a line hit.

When you overswing, you jerk your head and don't

see the ball real well, and, as a result, the fundamentals just aren't there. But if you concentrate and take a good, firm swing, everything falls into place.

Sometimes, a man will say, "I just tried to meet the ball and it went out of the park. How come?" Because he was waiting, almost as if he was going to take the pitch. Then, pow!

WHEN IT'S OKAY TO KILL

Even for a contact hitter, there are times when you should try to kill the ball. It will depend, of course, on the situation and your own abilities as a hitter.

Let's say you're a power hitter, the count is 3–1, and the team needs a run. If you get your pitch, by all means you should hit it as hard as you can. Sometimes you'll get the home run or at least an extra-base hit. If you miss the ball, the count is 3–2, and you can change to a more conservative swing on the next pitch, in order just to meet the ball and get on base. Under certain circumstances a singles hitter, too, should try to tee off on a pitch he likes.

There are times when I find I don't swing hard enough. Then I feel I might just as well go over to the sidelines and play pepper. When you're ahead of the pitcher, look for your pitch—and, if he gives it to you, try to cream it.

But remember, you can also be something of a hero without hitting the ball out of the ball park. You're a hero to your teammates in a different way by doing your job. If a man gets on base in the ninth inning, and you bunt him over so that the next man can knock him in, you've done what you've been asked to do. You've contributed to that winning score.

There are, of course, certain jobs within the batting order. The lead-off man's main responsibility is to get on base by hook or crook—by hit, by walk, or even by getting hit by the pitch. The second man is generally an outstanding hit-and-run man, a man who isn't likely to strike out and can hit behind the runner. He hits a lot of balls on the ground. The third, fourth, and fifth men are the power hitters, the men who can produce the runs, both by hitting homers and knocking other men in. This power trio, and usually the sixth man in the order and perhaps the seventh, will strike out more than the others, but they swing harder. The eighth man is someone who is not likely to strike out, and has the ability to get on base. The theory here is that, while pitchers are generally poor hitters, it would be possible for the pitcher to bunt the eighth man over if he should get on base to lead off an inning. Or, with two outs, the pitcher would probably make the last out, and the team would have the top of the order with which to start the next inning.

KNOWING YOUR PITCH

I talked before about hitting your pitch. What do I

Pulling the ball.

Hitting up the middle.

Hitting to the opposite field.

mean by *your* pitch? Simply, the kind *you* hit the best —the type, the speed, and the location you handle most effectively.

In the majors, a hitter faces a slider, curve, fastball, screwball, forkball, knuckleball, and spitball. There are innumerable variations, too, because different pitchers throw the same basic pitch differently.

A slider is really a flat curve. While a curve ball dips down, a slider curves to the side. But the slider some pitchers throw breaks down and away; it's really a roundhouse curve. One man throws a knuckleball so that it just sinks, while another pitcher throws it with a cutting motion so that it moves around.

HIT-AND-RUN

One of the prettiest plays in baseball is the hit-and-run. Actually, it's the run-and-hit because, essentially, the man should be running before you hit it.

The picture play is when the runner on first breaks for second, the second baseman runs over to cover, and the batter punches it through the hole vacated by the infielder for a base hit behind the runner.

That's the ideal hit-and-run, but it seldom happens. One reason is that the defensive team often anticipates the hit-and-run, so they'll throw outside to the left-handed hitter. If the batter tries to hit an outside pitch to right field, he'll probably pop it up.

On a hit-and-run, you should just try to hit the ball hard. Wait until you see where it is and then sock it. If it's inside, pull it; if it's outside, punch it. It's great if you can hit behind the runner, but often I've seen a man miss completely because he's changed his swing so drastically trying to do it.

There are men with good bat control like Jerry Grote who can wait to see which of the infielders is coming over to cover and—boom!—lace it through the opening. But the average player should just try to hit the ball, because if he does connect he's probably going to accomplish what the hit-and-run play is intended to do: first of all, get the runner from first into scoring position, and, if that fails, at least take away the chance for a double play.

For example, with the runner taking off for second, even if you hit a one-hop line shot right at the shortstop, and the second baseman is covering, your teammate may still make it safely to second anyway. Whether or not *you're* thrown out, you've got a man in scoring position. Whereas, chances are that, if you tried to hit behind the runner on an inside pitch (to a right-handed hitter), you'd probably hit an easy pop-up.

There are situations that cry out for hit-and-run, and the team in the field is going to do what it can to prevent it. But when the hit-and-run sign is flashed, you, as the batter, have the responsibility of trying to hit the ball no matter where it's pitched. You've got to protect the runner, so even if it's thrown over your head, just about, you've got to try to get at least a piece of the ball. Of course, if they throw a pitchout, I don't see any sense in making a wild swing that won't even touch the ball. They've simply outsmarted you, and you've got to swallow the consequences.

Incidentally, getting a piece of the ball, even on a pitch well out of the strike zone, shouldn't be that difficult—*if* you're waiting and you're ready for any type of pitch. Take a good look and react accordingly. If it's in, open up and hit it; if it's outside, go out and get it. In a hit-and-run situation you shouldn't be guessing, say, for an outside pitch so that you can hit behind the runner. If you do that and you get a ball up and in, you'll never handle it.

One of the reasons a man like Wayne Garrett hits so well on hit-and-run is that he waits so well. He can afford to wait because he's quick with the bat, and, as a result, he's tough to strike out and can spray his hits to all fields. Because they wait, you don't see the Wayne Garretts lunging after balls and missing them by a foot.

With some men up—Glenn Beckert, for instance— the team in the field can just about taste a hit-and-run coming, because he does the hit part so well. With others, they're not so sure.

Usually you hit-and-run when you're ahead of the pitcher. Say the count is 2 balls and 1 strike. The pitcher really doesn't want to go to 3–1, so the chances of a pitchout are reduced, and chances of a successful hit-and-run are increased. On the other hand, I've seen times when the count is 2–0 and there's been a pitchout, but the runner hasn't gone down. So it's 3–0. Maybe he comes in with the next pitch. The batter takes it, and still the runner holds. On 3–1 the pitcher can figure the runner will be going, but he can't very well pitch out. In fact, if he's too far off target, it's ball four—and the runner on first is moved to scoring position anyway.

THE SACRIFICE FLY

The time you really want to move a runner along is when he's already in scoring position. When you're looking for just one run and there's a man on third, a sacrifice fly is as good as a hit.

How do you go about hitting a sacrifice fly? Well, I know in my own case I really shouldn't try to hit a fly ball ever, even with a man on third base. I should just try to hit the ball hard.

That way, just by hitting up a little—usually on a ball that's close—I can get a fly ball or possibly a line drive. It's not a matter of hitting the ball farther than usual. They play me shallow anyway, so if I can get the ball up in the air and make them take a step back, it's tough for them to throw out the runner from third at the plate.

107

See, when the sacrifice fly isn't called for, everybody wants to hit line drives or balls on the ground. My swing is geared to hitting ground balls and I shouldn't change. In 1970 I had eight sacrifice flies, a club record, but I often got the ball into the air without trying to. If you try to hit the ball hard, you may get a base hit, which will surely get the runner in; if you don't connect solidly, you're likely to get the sacrifice fly. It's when you just try to make contact in that situation that you're probably going to hit an infield pop.

Here, too, you should wait for the pitch you handle best. Don't fish for anything that handcuffs you. I look for a ball in or down the middle, low, because that's the kind of pitch I can hit a fly ball on, if I don't get the base hit. If you get behind the pitcher, then you've got to hit his pitch. If he's got two strikes on you, then just pray you can hit the ball somewhere they can't get it.

CALLING THE PITCH: A GUESSING GAME

Willie Mays, one of the top three home-run hitters of all time, has socked more than 600 in his career. If they gave out assists on homers, Wes Westrum would have to be credited with about 100 of Willie's.

Wondrous Willie himself acknowledges that Westrum, who has been at different times Willie's manager, coach, and teammate, has called a lot of home-run pitches for him, flashing him signs on what to expect. Then Willie could set himself and uncork one of his out-of-the-park specialties.

Westrum does it, not so much by stealing catchers' signs, but by picking out little flaws or habits a pitcher has that give away what he's planning to throw. Maybe the pitcher moves his head a certain way when he's going to throw a curve. Westrum spots it, and signals ahead. He might yell, "Let's go," and Willie knows to expect a curve ball. Or he may say nothing, and Mays prepares for a fast ball.

Outside professional ball, it's not very often that a batter has advance notice of what pitch to expect. If he's lucky enough to have someone on the coaching lines who can let him know ahead of time what to expect, good for him. Of course, knowing isn't enough in itself. The batter has to be able to handle the pitches they're alerting him for.

This can backfire. A coach may think he sees a fast ball coming, lets his batter know, and then everyone is surprised by a curve ball. But you have to be willing to be fooled, if necessary, and take chances at the plate. You can't play everything safe or think defensively while you're hitting. You have to be aggressive. And, in order to be aggressive, you have to guess.

Once the pitcher gets ahead of you, you should play it safe. But until he does, you have every reason in the world to take chances and guess what pitch is coming, fast ball or breaking ball, and whether it will be in or out. If you're wrong, you're wrong. You're not dead yet—not until the last strike.

Having said all this, I want to caution against *too much* guessing, especially when you're young. You'll do fine if you wait to see the pitch and then go get it. That way, your chances of getting base hits are a lot better than those of the fellow who guesses but commits himself too soon. Say he's guessed that a ball is coming inside and he begins moving into it. But the pitcher has thrown a good pitch down and away and, because the batter has already committed his stride and his hands, he can't handle the pitch. He'll either have to take it or swing awkwardly and be lucky to get a piece of it.

BUNTING

There are two basic kinds of bunts—the sacrifice bunt, when you're prepared to make an out so that a runner can advance to scoring position, and the bunt for a base hit.

Bunting looks a lot easier than it is—especially if you're trying to do it when everybody expects it. In that circumstance, the pitcher will be throwing to make you pop the ball up, and the first and third basemen will be charging down your throat. You've got to stay cool and do what you're supposed to do.

To bunt you have to, in effect, play catch with the bat—hold it almost as if it were a glove waiting to receive the ball. As the pitcher delivers, you quickly slide your top hand up to the fat part of the bat, up near the trademark, grasping it lightly with your thumb on top and four fingers underneath. The bottom hand stays where it is, firmly grasping the bat, knuckles toward the pitcher. That lower hand determines the angle of the bunt. Be sure the fingers of your top hand are not around the front of the bat—that's dangerous.

As you move your hand, you're moving your body into bunt position. When you're trying a sacrifice bunt, just before the pitcher releases the ball, swing your body around to face him. You can do this in one of several ways. If you stand close to the plate, pivot your back foot to face the pitcher and move your front foot back even with it. A player who stands away from the plate should pivot on his front foot, and bring his back foot up even. Some players prefer to move both feet— the front foot away from the plate and the back foot up even with the front foot.

As you await the pitch, it might be best to keep the bat level around the top of your strike zone. If the pitch comes in lower, you can dip from the waist and knees to meet it.

The arm of your top hand should be kept about parallel with the ground, and both arms should be bent at the elbows. You should be slightly crouched, with your weight a bit forward. The bat has to be in front of

Sacrifice bunt. Keep the bat out where you can see it, which is why the bat here looks so big.

Wrong—the bat is too far back.

A bunt to the third baseman. You turn the bat in that direction, but it is still out in front where you can see it.

you, where you can see it. And don't push at the ball. Let the ball hit the bat, and the arms and hands will take the impact.

Bunting for a base hit is a different story. Since surprise is a major element, you don't want to give away your intention until the last possible moment. The same thing applies when you're trying to squeeze in a runner from third. In that case, you don't want to get into bunt position until the pitcher has committed himself; that way, he can't change his plan and throw it down and away for the catcher to make the tag. So you wait until, in his motion, the pitcher has reached the point of no return.

When you're going to bunt for a base hit, you hold the bat a little tighter and you actually meet the ball while on the move. A right-handed hitter can either dump the ball down the third-base line or push it past the pitcher on the first-base side, so that either the second baseman or first baseman, playing deep, will have to field it.

For a left-handed hitter, a natural place to try for a bunt hit is down the first-base line—actually dragging the ball as he starts running for first. This is called a *drag bunt*.

Footwork is different on a bunt for a hit than on a sacrifice bunt, since you're waiting longer. You take a step *into* the pitch as you dump, push, or drag it.

When you're at the plate, it's essential to be alert to your coach's signs to bunt, because, if you're not pay-

Here is a good position for executing a drag bunt. Your back foot should move directly toward the pitcher and the bat must be in front of you. You must be able to see the ball hit the bat.

A bad way to drag the ball. The foot is raised and the bat is back too far. You cannot see it make contact with the ball.

ing attention, your teammates on the base paths could be dead ducks.

If you should miss the sign, it's best to do what Bob Robertson of the Pirates did against the Orioles in the seventh inning of the third game of the 1971 World Series. There were two men on and the bunt sign was flashed to him. He didn't see it, and instead hit a three-run homer for a 5–1 Pittsburgh victory.

DRAWING WALKS

Like stealing third or home, drawing walks is just a matter of judgment. "Get a walk" isn't something your coach can order, although you can, to a degree, help it happen.

The fellows who are the best at it are those with the quick bats who can afford to wait till the last possible instant to see whether they swing at the pitch or let it go. The longer you wait on a pitch, the better chance you have of seeing whether it's a ball or a strike.

When I'm right, I draw a lot of walks. In the 1970 season I did, but not in 1971, partly because the pitchers were challenging me more. They weren't just trying to make me hit bad pitches or pitch around me. On 3–2, they'd try to throw on the corner or pitch one that was too close to the plate to risk taking.

Very often, late in the game a manager will order a batter to take a pitch, especially someone like me, someone they want on base so the hitters that follow can drive him in. And if the pitcher doesn't seem to be throwing well, "take" signs may be given earlier in the game.

4. Running the Bases

A s s o o n a s you hit the ball, you become a base runner, a potential score for your team. Make the most of it.

Base running is, more than anything, instinct. But there are ways to sharpen that instinct, ways in which hustle can more than make up for limited speed.

Whether you hit a pop-up, grounder, or deep line drive—even if it looks like a sure out—take off for first base as quickly as you can. The same holds true if the ball gets past the catcher on ball four or strike three. (Years ago, when Brooklyn Dodger catcher Mickey Owen couldn't hold onto a strike-three pitch to New York Yankees outfielder Tommy Henrich in the ninth inning of a World Series game the Dodgers were winning, Henrich legged it safely to first and started a rally that led to a Yankee victory.)

When you make your turn at first base, touch the corner of the base so you can push off. You should swing into the base so you come in at an angle.

Getting a fast start from the batter's box is essential. Some experts recommend starting on one foot or the other, but I think you should start whatever way comes naturally, without thinking about it. And as you hustle down the line, try to watch what's happening. If you hit the ball to the right side, it's all there in front of you; if you hit the ball to the left side, just a glance over the shoulder will keep you informed.

If it shapes up as a squeaker play at first base, keep going at top speed across the bag (and then turn to the right, to foul territory, and come back to the base, unless the throw goes wild). But on any kind of sure base hit, be ready to take an extra base by making a turn toward second. This is best done by swinging to your right a little before approaching first from the foul side. Try to hit the inside corner of the bag with either foot. You round the bag, go partway toward second, then stop and look. If the ball is deep, or the outfielder bobbles it, and you think you can make it to second, give it a go. You've got to take chances in baserunning. But not foolish chances. You watch out for the right fielder you know likes to throw back to first behind the runner, and you don't make a mad dash for second against the fielder with the crackerjack arm who is coming in on the ball. If there's no chance of making it to second, you hustle back to first.

Like good hitting or fielding, good baserunning depends a lot on concentration. It's not a simple matter of you being on first and, when the batter hits the ball, racing to second. There's much more involved. You have to remind yourself of such possibilities as line drives being hit directly at a fielder, so you can't be too anxious to go. On fly balls you have to learn—from experience—when it's wise to go halfway to the next base on the chance the ball will drop in, or when it's wiser to be tagging up, ready to take off the instant the ball is caught.

As much as you have to keep your wits about you and make your own decisions on the base paths, you have to rely a great deal on coaches. Suppose you're on first and the ball is hit right down the first-base line.

You can't very well run down to second and be looking back over your shoulder. You have to depend on the third-base coach to tell you whether you've got a chance of making it safely to third.

Similarly, on a ball you hit down the third-base line, you may not be able to follow the play as you run. If I'm not following the ball myself, I'll put my head down and watch Yogi Berra, our first-base coach, for a "go-ahead" sign to try to make it into a double.

The coach shouldn't have to make up your mind for you if you can see the play unfold in front of you, such as when you're on first base and the ball is hit down the left-field line. But there are instances, as I've noted, when either the ball is in a bad position for you to look, or it's hit where you'd have to slow down to get the picture. Then you depend on the coach.

With or without direction from the coach, you've got to be aggressive on the base paths. You never assume that the man is going to field the ball cleanly, and that's why you hustle down to first and take a wide turn. If you got there in a hurry, you'll be in a good position to move on if he boots it. You've got the momentum and it's easy to keep going. But if you were hesitant and cautious, you'll never make it unless the ball goes right through the outfielder. You can turn singles into doubles and doubles into triples by aggressive running, and sometimes your hustle can force fielders into making errors. Players like Pete Rose, who's called "Charley Hustle," look as if they're going to second on a walk. On a hit, you know they'll take an extra base on the slightest fielding lapse.

But remember, there are times when caution pays off. It's senseless to make a big turn toward second when the man is standing there ready to put the tag on you.

When you're on base, don't take a lead until the pitcher steps on the rubber and you know he has the ball. Even in the major leagues, every once in a while, someone comes up with the hidden-ball trick. The runner thinks the pitcher has the ball and takes his lead, but all the time the fielder has it and easily puts the tag on him. So be aggressive, but be careful.

SLIDING

A good slide can often spell the difference between safe and out.

Surprisingly, there are major-league players who don't like to slide, either because they don't have the coordination, or (in the case of pitchers, who don't get on base often) the experience.

Some players are concerned about the dangers of sliding. You *can* get hurt, but not if you follow instructions.

The best way to practice is with your shoes off. Never attempt to work on your sliding wearing shoes or spikes, because, if you're in the process of learning, you're probably still uncoordinated doing it. If you're not coordinated, you may jump and hook your spikes into the ground, and maybe sprain or even break an ankle.

I recommend you practice on grass, because that's a surface you can actually slide on and not come up with any strawberry bruises, as you can on dirt that's a little bit hard.

In spring training we put on a pair of football pants, take off our shoes, and slide on grass.

There are three basic recommended slides: the hook, the straight-in and the bent-leg.

One not recommended is the head-first slide, in which you belly-wop into the bag, with your hands stretched out ahead of you. Frank Robinson slid safely into third that way on Merv Rettenmund's single in the tenth inning of the sixth game of the 1971 World Series. (Then, on Brooks Robinson's sacrifice fly, Frank used a bent-leg slide to score the Orioles' winning run.) I used a head-first slide for a while because it seemed to be faster and allowed me to start my slide earlier, but I don't any more—and *I wouldn't recommend it for anyone any time.* The reason I'm so dead set against it is that it is extremely dangerous. You're going in with bare hands in front of you; your head is exposed, and, if the man covering the base drops his knee in front of the bag, you may jam your fingers or break your neck.

Yes, there are players who use it, but for you to try

Front and side views of a head-first slide. This is the fastest of the slides, since you're running with your body bent, and it's quick just to fall at the base. But be aware of the dangers to hands, fingers, and head.

The hook slide shown here is a variation of the straight-in slide, used to avoid a fielder's tag. The difference is that here you must hook your foot around the corner of the base.

to copy it is like trying to jump backwards the way Dick Fosbury, the Olympics champion high-jumper, did. *He* knew how to do it, but his imitators didn't, and some got seriously hurt.

The hook slide is valuable to have in your bag of baserunning tricks for use on special occasions, such as when the fielder is on one side of the bag and you want to go in on the other. You just slide past the bag, and hook it with your underneath foot. The drawback is that, while it looks fancy and is often effective, you've lost that much distance going past the bag to one side, compared with sliding straight in.

There's no reason to use the hook on a force play, since you want to get to the base as quickly as possible. Use it only when you're trying to avoid a tag. Say you're trying to slide around the catcher—or, on a ground ball, suppose the throw to first was high enough to pull the first baseman off the bag. You know he's going to come down for you straight on the bag, so you go to the outside.

All in all, though, a slide in which you come straight into the bag is usually the fastest and most effective. On a steal I always use it, no matter where the throw comes.

Ideally, you should be able to slide on either side of yourself, but, as with hitting, most players slide a lot better on one side than the other. I favor my right. It would be nice to be versatile, to be able to slide on one side or the other, but I can still adjust when I have to by sliding on my right side to the left side of the base and grabbing for the bag with my hand.

When you decide to slide, don't change your mind, or you'll be in trouble.

Before you go into your slide, approach the base with your body fairly erect and your gaze fixed on the bag. Experience will teach you how far from the base you should begin your slide, whatever the type.

The bent-leg and straight-in (or "feet-first," as it's sometimes called) are essentially the same. The only difference is that in the bent-leg you take off into your fall closer to the bag, your extended leg is bent more at

This is a bent-leg slide, a type of slide I recommend. It is the most direct route to the base. As the top leg reaches toward the bag, your underneath leg should be bent.

the knee, and the top part of your body is kept straighter. In the feet-first, both feet are extended toward the base.

For any of the recommended slides, take off on either foot, depending on which feels more natural. If you slide on your right hip, bend your right leg under you and keep the left foot up, reaching for the base. Keep your bent leg turned sideways, so the spikes don't get caught in the dirt.

When you slide properly, you hit the ground high on the buttocks, near the hip. You're actually sitting back and bringing your legs up, so that your weight is back, resembling a kind of cradle. The upper part of your body will go backwards, but you're not on your back or the back of your head. The bent leg takes the impact of your fall and you slide on it, until your other leg, the extended one, touches the bag.

In the hook slide, one or both knees may be bent and both feet turned sideways to avoid catching spikes in the ground. If I'm hooking, I slide on my right side, keep my right leg bent and my left leg straight. I hook with my left foot. Others have their left leg bent and their right leg straight. It's all a matter of personal preference.

Whichever way you slide, you should try to get up as quickly as you can, to take another base if, say, the throw goes wild. It helps to push up on the bent leg as your forward leg touches the bag. The momentum will have you standing at once. Players who slide low on their backs just keep sliding, and, if the ball goes into center field, they can't get up in time to take advantage of it.

I have a habit of putting my right hand back when I'm sliding, so that I can push off and get up even more quickly, but that's not a recommended sliding procedure. In fact, for a while I kept dirt in my hands when I led off from first as a reminder not to put the hand back.

BREAKING UP THE DOUBLE PLAY

It's understood that when you're heading for second

127

on an attempted double play, you try to break up the play. What you *don't* do is try to kick the ball out of the fielder's hands. You don't want to go in and disable him so he has no more career.

How do you take a man out of the play without hurting him? Well, since I don't have the weight to take his weight out, I just try to disturb him enough so he leaves his feet. If I can slide in there, I just nudge him with my shin, and the fielder, feeling something hit his leg, is instinctively going to lift it back up. If you can get him to leave his feet so he can't throw on to first accurately, then you've done your job—you've taken him out. Sometimes, just making him *think* you're going to take him out is enough. In the 1971 National League play-offs, the Giants' second baseman, Tito Fuentes, made a force play at second, but then just about lobbed the ball to first and missed the double play. The speculation was that he had set himself in the expectation that the runner was going to plow into him. When the runner didn't, it affected Tito's rhythm.

Trying to kick the ball out of a fielder's glove on a tag play is also dangerous, and I don't like to do it. If you come in straight and he drops his glove so that it hooks your shoe and the ball comes out, that's one thing. But it's quite another to use your spikes to kick it out. Those dangerous weapons on your feet can cut up a man pretty badly. So I don't use my spikes—or my knee, for that matter.

There's one situation where it's acceptable to put

128

your entire body into play at the expense of a fielder. That's when you're trying to score and the catcher has the plate blocked so thoroughly that even a hook slide won't get you around him. In that case it's your privilege—at your own risk—to slam into him and maybe jar the ball loose. Remember Pete Rose and Ray Fosse in the 1969 All-Star game?

STEALING

A lot more than pure speed enters into successful base thievery. Headwork counts as much as footwork.

In a way, stealing bases begins in the dugout. As I mentioned earlier, bases are stolen on the pitcher rather than on the catcher. The key, then, is spotting something about the pitcher that will tip you off on whether or not he's going to be throwing over to hold you to first base.

When you're in the dugout and a teammate is on first, put yourself mentally into the baserunner's shoes and consider: "If I were the man on first and I were going to steal, what would I look for?"

You might study the pitcher's feet, his shoulders or head, to see what he does differently when he's about to throw over to first, as compared to when he's just going to proceed with his pitch. If you can spot a flaw, a giveaway sign that telegraphs his intention, you've got that much of an edge when you're on base. Then you'll be able to say to yourself, "Well, he's not coming over this time," and off you go. You may be crossed up, too, and be picked off, but usually you've read the situation correctly and you've got the base stolen easily.

Some young players think that a big lead is all-important in stealing a base. A good jump is critical, but it's my philosophy that you should take the same lead all the time—whether you're planning to steal or not. That way, *you* won't be guilty of a giveaway sign of *your* intention.

Obviously, if you were always to take a short lead when you're not going and a long lead when you are, the opposition would always know when to throw over or pitch out. Some runners telegraph their intentions so clearly, by movement of their hands or feet, the opposition doesn't even bother throwing over. The hurler just pitches out and they're caught with ease.

So take the same kind of lead all the time. A safe lead off first is a turn and a dive—which means that, if the pitcher throws over suddenly, you can get back just by turning and diving. I like to take a lead that's a step and a half and a dive away from the bag. That's not quite as safe as the turn and dive, but it's a distance I can handle—and it also gives me sufficient jump to beat a catcher's throw to second.

If you want to be ready for any eventuality, lead off with your weight evenly balanced so you can go in either direction with equal ease. And, when you take your lead, stay on a straight line between first and sec-

Leading off base. Line up straight with second base and keep yourself balanced so you can go either way.

ond so you don't cost yourself the extra steps that would be required if you set out on a roundabout course.

In the 1971 season I had twenty-eight steals out of thirty-four attempts. Part of that high percentage of success is due, I think, to *wanting* to go. Often, I've had the sign to steal but felt I hadn't a good enough jump, and so didn't go, thereby probably preventing being cut down. I get the type of sign that allows me to steal on any pitch I want, while a particular hitter is at the plate. If, for some reason, the manager decides against a steal attempt, the coach will signal me that the sign is being taken off.

Almost always, my attempts at stealing second come on a sign rather than on my own initiative. Stealing third or home is a different matter, because of the element of surprise involved, so you try that entirely on your own.

Trying to steal home can be dangerous, in more ways than one. Remember the 1969 National League playoff between the Braves and the Mets? Tommie Agee tried to steal home and almost had his head taken off by a line foul shot off the bat of Cleon Jones.

Usually, though, the danger is in being thrown out. During the 1971 season, in a night game against the Padres, we had the bases loaded and two outs. I was halfway down the line at third and decided to take a chance and come all the way. The trouble was that the pitcher spotted me in time and easily caught me at home. It's a situation where you're either a goat or a hero, and you can figure out which I was for that play. But if the same situation were to arise again, I might very well break for home if I thought the element of surprise, the jump I had, and other conditions made the odds right.

You have to take chances—when the chances are worth taking. Say you're on second with one out. If you feel the batter is a good enough fly-ball hitter to get you in on a sacrifice fly from third, it may be worth trying to steal third.

There are times when, in effect, you offer to sacrifice yourself—as a runner. An example of that is when there's a man on second and you come through with a single. If it looks as if there's a good chance they're going to be able to nail him at home, you head for second. What you hope to do is encourage the defensive team to cut off the ball and try to nab you at second. If they do, fine, because you've made sure the runner has scored. On the other hand, if they still throw home, you're then in potential scoring position. The same strategy might even apply with two outs, except that you'd make sure you didn't get tagged out at second until your teammate had crossed the plate.

A Final Word
from Bud

IN THIS BOOK I've tried to offer suggestions on how to sharpen your skills so you become a better baseball player and enjoy the game more.

It's in no way an attempt to give *all* the answers. No book is big enough, and no man is smart enough, to do that. And I want to emphasize again that you have to adapt the suggestions that *are* here to your individual style and ability.

There are, however, basic principles that apply to everyone, big or little, raw rookie or seasoned veteran. Boiled down to a sentence, they say: Learn your capabilities, develop your God-given talents, many or few; practice constantly, especially on your weaknesses; concentrate; use your head; hustle—and enjoy yourself.

134

If you remember these points alone, the book will have done its job. The rest will come on the playing field.

Glossary

AHEAD OF THE COUNT. When the batter has fewer strikes on him than balls, he is said to be ahead of the count.

ASSIST. Fielding credit given when a defensive player throws or deflects a batted or thrown ball so that a putout results (or if a putout would have resulted if an error didn't follow). An example would be the man who starts the double play. The pivot man gets credit for both a putout and an assist.

BASE STICKER. A runner who stays very close to the base.

BASKET CATCH. A catch in which the hands are cupped against the body to form a "basket."

BATTER'S BOX. A six-by-four-foot lined-off area on either side of the plate, where the batter must stay while hitting.

BEHIND THE COUNT. When the batter has more strikes called on him than balls, he is said to be behind the count.

BEHIND THE RUNNER. When a man is on base, the batter will often try to hit to right field—behind where the runner is headed.

BENT-LEG SLIDE. A slide in which one leg is bent under the one that reaches for the bag. It can be aimed directly at the bag or to the side.

BLOOP HIT. A soft liner or fly ball that just manages to drop in for a base hit.

BREAKING PITCH. A pitch that changes direction as it comes across the plate.

BULLPEN. An area in foul territory where relief pitchers warm up.

BUNT. A batted ball placed in the infield, usually close to the foul lines and near home plate, in an attempt to sacrifice a runner or get a base hit.

CHOKING UP ON THE BAT. When a hitter holds his bat several inches from the bottom, he is said to be choking up on the bat.

CONTACT HITTER. A batsman who makes contact with the ball and is content to hit singles rather than swing hard for distance.

COUNT. The number of balls and strikes on a batter.

CROWDING THE PLATE. When a batter stands very

close to home plate, he is said to be crowding it.

CUTOFF. Interception of a throw, usually from the out-field, by an infielder other than the one for whom the throw is intended.

DEAD HANDS. When a batter holds his bat still, instead of moving his hands back so he can better pro-pel his bat, he is said to have "dead hands."

DIAMOND. The shape of the infield bounded by the four bases, including home plate. Also refers to the entire playing area.

DRAG BUNT. A bunt in which the left-handed batter drags the ball along as he runs toward first base.

DUGOUT. The area provided for each team to sit, usu-ally under the stands, between home plate and first base and between home and third base.

FLY BALL. A ball hit high into the air.

GRASS-CUTTER. A ground ball that hugs the grass.

HANDCUFFED. When a batter can't swing smoothly because a pitch is thrown in very close to him, he is said to be handcuffed. Similarly, a bad hop may handcuff a fielder.

HANDLE. When a fielder can't get a grip on a ball, it's said he can't find the "handle."

HEAD-FIRST SLIDE. A slide in which, arms extended, the weight of the body is thrown toward the bag. Not recommended because of danger.

HOOK SLIDE. A slide in which the runner slides past the bag, to the side, with toe hooking the base as he goes by. Sometimes a hand is used to hook the bag.

HIT-AND-RUN. An offensive play in which the base runner breaks with the pitch and the batter tries to hit the ball. Often he tries to hit it through an opening in the infield, sometimes the hole left by the fielder coming in to cover the base where the runner is heading. The batter must swing and try to get a piece of the ball to protect his running teammate.

HOT CORNER. Third base, so called because a ball hit down there sizzles.

INFIELD FLY RULE. A rule that prevents a fielder from deliberately dropping a pop fly in the infield in order to make a force-out double play. The rule applies when there are less than two outs and there are men on first and second, or on all the bases, and the fielder is in a reasonable position to catch the ball. Whether he catches it or not, the batter is ruled out automatically. The runner may move at his own risk.

JAMMING. When a pitch is thrown in very close to the hitter, preventing him from swinging smoothly, he is being jammed.

JUMP. A base runner's getaway lead for an attempted stolen base.

LEAD. The distance a runner stands from the base. Also, the score by which a team is winning.

LEAD-OFF MAN. The first man in a team's batting order. Also, the first man up for a team in an inning.

LEAD RUNNER. The runner closest to home. If, for instance, there are men on first and third, the man on third is the lead runner.

LETTER HIGH. Referring to a pitch that crosses the plate below the batter's shoulders, about the level of the letters on the player's uniform.

LOLLIPOP. Ballplayers' term for a ball that's thrown too softly.

MOUND. The raised, circular dirt area where the pitcher stands.

OPPOSITE FIELD HITTER. A right-handed hitter who hits to the right side of second base, or a left-handed hitter who hits to the left side—in other words, opposite of their "power" fields.

OVERHAND. A pitch or throw made with the throwing arm straight up, near the ear.

PALM BALL. A throw made with the ball touching the thrower's palm. Usually this kind of throw has to be pushed out.

PASSED BALL. A pitched ball that the catcher fails to stop that he should have, and which allows a runner to advance.

PEPPER GAME. Warm-up exercise in which a batter bunts to his teammates, who immediately "pitch" the ball back to him for another bunt.

PICK-OFF. When a base runner is caught off base for a putout.

PITCHOUT. When a pitcher throws the ball well outside the batter's range so the catcher can throw down to a base and try to pick off a runner or stop him from stealing.

PIVOT MAN. The fielder who makes the first putout of an attempted double play.

PLATOONING. A player who is in the lineup against certain opposition, such as a right-handed pitcher, but is benched against others, is said to be platooned.

POP FLY. A high fly ball in or not far beyond the infield.

PULL HITTER. A right-handed batter who hits to the left side of the field, or a left-handed batter who hits to the right side.

PUSH BUNT. A bunt by a right-handed batter between the pitcher and first baseman, too deep for the pitcher to field.

RBI (RUN BATTED IN). A batter is credited with an RBI when his base hit, walk, or out is responsible for a teammate scoring. Also, if he's hit by a pitch with the bases loaded, and, in certain situations, if he's safe on an error. He does *not* get RBI credit if he hits into a force double play or one started by the first baseman stepping on first base.

RELAY. When a ball is thrown from an outfielder to another player, who immediately throws it on to a third teammate.

ROOKIE. A new player. Someone in his first year in a league.

RUBBER. The slab on the pitching mound the pitcher must touch with one foot as he delivers his pitch.

RUNDOWN. A play in which defensive players move to tag out a runner caught between bases.

SACRIFICE. A ball hit by the batter to advance a runner in such a way that the batter will almost surely be out, either a fly ball on which the runner scores after the ball is caught or a bunt.

SCORING POSITION. The position a base runner on second or third base is considered to be in, in case of a base hit.

SCREWBALL. A pitch that drifts and dips and turns with the wind en route to the plate.

SIDEARM. A pitch or throw delivered with the arm extended to the side.

SINKER BALL. A fast ball that drops as it comes near the plate.

SINKING LINE DRIVE. A batted ball that drops rapidly.

SLIDER. A fast ball that slides to the side of its original path as it approaches the plate.

SOUTHPAW. A left-handed thrower or batter.

SPRAY HITTER. A man who hits to all fields.

STRAIGHT-AWAY HITTER. A batter who tends to hit the ball to center field, or in an area somewhere between left center and right center.

STRAIGHT-IN SLIDE. A feet-first slide in which both

legs are extended toward the bag.

SUBMARINE. A pitch or throw delivered underhand.

SWITCH-HITTER. A batter who is capable of hitting the ball from either side of the plate.

TAGGING UP. The act of a runner touching the base he's on as a fly ball is caught, in preparation for an attempt at advancing to the next base. Can happen only with less than two out.

TAKE SIGN. A signal given to a batter to let the next pitch go by without swinging at it.

THREE-QUARTERS. A pitch or throw delivered with the arm somewhere between the sidearm and overhand positions.

BUD HARRELSON

Born in Niles, California, Bud Harrelson signed with the New York Mets as a freshman out of San Francisco State College in 1963. After a few years in the minors, Bud became the Mets' regular shortstop and played a key role in the spectacular National League pennant and World Series victories in 1969. In 1970, when he tied a league record for most consecutive errorless games for a shortstop (54), and in 1971, he was the National League's All-Star Shortstop. He lives with his wife and two children in East Northport, New York. In the off season, Bud relaxes with golf and club dates as a country singer.

JOEL H. COHEN

Joel H. Cohen is a free-lance writer whose books include biographies of Hank Aaron, Johnny Unitas, Kareem Jabbar (Lew Alcindor), and the Van Arsdale twins.